The Research-Ready Classroom

Differentiating Instruction WITHDRAW
Across Content Areas

Mike Anderson and Andy Dousis

HEINEMANN
Portsmouth, NH

Heinemann
361 Hanover Street
Portsmouth, NH 03801–3912
www.heinemann.com

Offices and agents throughout the world

© 2006 by Mike Anderson and Andy Dousis

Library of Congress Cataloging-in-Publication Data
Anderson, Mike.
　The research-ready classroom : differentiating instruction across content areas /
　　Mike Anderson and Andy Dousis.
　　　p.　cm.
　Includes bibliographical references.
　ISBN 0-325-00944-9 (alk. paper)
　1. Research—Methodology—Study and teaching (Elementary).
2. Individualized instruction.　3. Content area reading.　　I. Dousis, Andy.
II. Title.

LB1047.3.A63 2006
372.139′4—dc22　　　　　　　　　　　　　　　　　2005031481

Editor: Thomas Newkirk
Production: Elizabeth Valway
Cover design: Night & Day Design
Composition: Reuben Kantor, QEP Design
Manufacturing: Jamie Carter

Printed in the United States of America on acid-free paper
10 09 08　　　EB　　　3 4 5

We dedicate this book to all of our teachers, both young and old.

Contents

Foreword: Gifts

The Research-Ready Classroom is a guide, a manual, and a gift—in fact, several gifts. It is a critical alternative to the test-weary state of classrooms today. The authors, Mike Anderson and Andy Dousis, experienced and masterful teachers, guide us through a challenging curriculum. They pack each chapter with instruction; they share strategies, activities, resources, and anecdotes illustrating many of the techniques that help children learn best. And importantly, their approach restores what is really the central project of education—the task of kindling in children an earnest desire to learn. Unfortunately, in today's classrooms, teachers as well as their students have less and less say. Curriculum is often mandated by district, state, or national requirements; decisions are imposed from above; and beyond that, site-based initiatives that actually work are frequently confounded, frustrated, and even thwarted. Thus, we are in need of inspiration, frequent infusions of courage, and the practical skills to sustain this calling to educate—gifts I found reading this book.

Years ago, I learned about the research project curriculum Mike and Andy were developing when I was invited to see their classrooms. It was summer and only the artifacts from a previous semester, cloaked in the heat and dust, were available to view. And yet despite the museumlike silence, within moments we could almost hear the buzz of children exploring a rain-forest habitat, looking over a papier-mâché polar bear, or creating an illustrated chart about baseball. As these teachers recalled the projects, the wonderful energy of the classroom returned as did the sheer accomplishments they oversaw. Fortunately, these teachers were willing to share their accrued knowledge. And it so needs to be shared. Of course, in the summer, without the actual intrusion of twenty-plus students, it is easy to romanticize, not to imagine the mess, demands, time pressures, and challenging behaviors. But what is clear from their reports is that years of honing and crafting yielded a realistic approach to the research process. Mike and Andy were learning how to structure and scaffold, integrate social and academic objectives, and teach skills proactively with opportunities for modeling and practicing. From topic to final presentation they have framed carefully sequenced steps that make the concepts and skills transparent even for new teachers. Of course, after reading this book, I see many of the reasons why my own attempts to do research projects with twenty-five students backfired; I even start to envision how I might go back and teach just one more year. I am that excited—almost!

The capacity to teach discipline is key to this approach. John Dewey, in *Experience and Education,* wrote that "The ultimate aim of education is creation of the powers of self-control" (1998, 64). The powers of self-control are realized in the ability to frame purposes and follow through. These powers take hold the more we can translate curiosity and impulse into "intelligent activity." Without the impetus and fuel of curiosity, however, students will not have the resolve to overcome frustration and problems. The authors, Mike and Andy, write in their introduction, "They are invested in the work because it is *their* work." "Their work," the topics ignited by children's own desires, combine with a structure established by their teachers. It is this combination (student choices and rigorous, knowing teacher facilitation), too often lacking in our current school agendas, that provides our best chance to encourage achievement and disciplined learning. The tools to succeed, the specific skills required, are precisely identified and addressed so that curiosity becomes creation.

The potentials for constructive learning are embedded in the rigors of this approach to doing research with children. I recall taking a fifth-grade class on a field trip many years ago when we were doing a river study. Despite wonderful guides and fascinating terrain, most of the attention was on boots, lunch, and partners. Students observed little and gathered even less knowledge about why rivers meander or what created the steep cliff sides. I realized, after the fact, that I had sent them off without the proper tools. They had no questions to excite their interest; nothing to anticipate and to wonder about that compelled exploration (not counting who sat behind them on the bus!). The next time we did take a trip, questions were their ticket and the results improved.

How to help children develop their own good questions is the meat of Chapter 5. Mike and Andy show the importance of good questions, but they do not assume that children know how to create them. Instead, Mike and Andy are prepared to teach the skills. They illustrate a number of different techniques: modeling self-questioning, brainstorming in small groups, having partner chats, working with inside/outside circles, journaling, and more. Children learn by listening to one another, conferring with teachers, and practicing. At each step of the way, the objectives are explicit and the instruction varied and rich.

Another example: Early on in the term children choose a topic for their research study. Initially, the authors tell us, the topic may grow out of the social studies themes, with more open-ended options later on in the year. In either case, we know that students do not automatically make appropriate choices. When teaching third graders, I quickly learned that they had a tendency to think in epic terms with casts of thousands and projects that could last a century. My sixth graders, on the other hand, could procrastinate forever, checking out the "coolness quotient" of every idea! Some children had a hard time locating their own interests. Some had only the vaguest notions and ended up with generalities. In Chapter 4, "Topic Selection," the authors describe a vital process to explore potential choices. They show ways to "spark interest" and to brainstorm as a group with such interesting strategies as "inside/outside circles" as a method to help children better define their topics. They also describe numbers of ways to help children narrow and focus their topics on the essential questions they most want to know. There is the story of a student who pondered her topic all summer, full of delicious anticipation to begin third grade. And another one who assigned and directed the research projects of a younger sibling over her summer!

At each step, throughout each chapter, we learn ways to engage and stretch learning. It applies to a research curriculum, but it is what invigorates all good practice. We will be better teachers whatever the subject.

"These things don't just happen automatically," the authors point out, referring perhaps to how children make appropriate choices or work cooperatively, plan their work period, gather meaningful source materials, decipher an index, or measure poster boards for neat displays. Thus, each component is richly grounded in realistic and practical management strategies. The results are deliberate and sequential. They are organized around clearly framed goals with useful illustrations about how to prioritize objectives so that expectations do not overwhelm either children or teacher.

Again, this is a book that delivers on its title, but it also reinvigorates good practice. It shows us how to construct a process that begins with the children, honors their individual interests, and scaffolds the skills. It establishes continuous accountability with user-friendly record-keeping systems and even peer-group check-ins. It is applicable to all we teach across the grades and content areas. It makes manageable the juggling act that is the balance of the individual interests and range of aptitudes in a classroom community. When I used to try to do research projects on individual topics with my students, I quickly found myself flooded in detail and pulled in a zillion directions. It was too much, and so I pared it down further and further until there were fewer choices and lower expectations. Learning from the work of Andy and Mike, I see now how to set realistic goals and develop skills with simple intention. It almost makes me want to go back to school and anticipate, like their students, my first research project. I think it might be on starfish or perhaps the native peoples of New Zealand. How will I ever choose—can I do both?

—Ruth Charney, Senior Consultant
Northeast Foundation for Children
Turners Falls, Massachusetts

Acknowledgments

We would like to acknowledge the professional support and guidance of the people of the Northeast Foundation for Children, a dedicated and passionate group of educators who are reshaping American schools through the teachings of the Responsive Classroom.

We would also like to thank Tom Newkirk for his encouragement to work on this book. Without his help and expertise, it never would have happened.

1

Introduction

My class of fifth graders moves purposely from the class meeting area to their workspaces. Dominique and Tim go straight for the paint supplies and lay down newspaper on the counter. TJ, Rico, and Kathryn sit at a table and begin rifling through their notes to see what information they still need to gather. Three other children sign out of the classroom on a mini dry-erase board to head for the computer room. One of them is working on a PowerPoint presentation on foxes, another is typing a poem about Jackie Robinson, while the third is meeting with the computer teacher to search the Internet for more websites about the Battle of Gettysburg. In a corner of the room, I meet with four students at a round table to help facilitate a discussion. Three of them feel like they have enough facts about their various topics to move on to working on their projects, but they need to check in with each other to make sure. The fourth is looking for some help. He can't find any information about the childhood of Michael Jordan, even though he seems to have the right books. One of his peers suggests he look in the table of contents, and together the group finds the chapter he needs.

All around the room, students are engaged in their work. Each student is different. They have different cultural backgrounds, are at different developmental levels, participate in different after-school activities, and have different families. Each student is studying a topic of his or her choice, yet meeting several different curricular objectives set by our district for the students' grade level in multiple content areas. They are even preparing for the upcoming state standardized tests.

What's most important about this scene is the energy level and enthusiasm of the students. Kids move about the room with purpose. When they enter the room in the morning and see the schedule posted, the first thing they look for is the research period. Throughout work periods, students chat excitedly about their learning. "Whoa! Did you know that the largest spider in the world is eleven inches across! It can catch mice and birds!" exclaims a student with a mixture of fascination and horror. Other students nearby lean in to catch a glimpse of the monster spider and with a shudder, turn back to their books. At a nearby table, a student questions another: "How did you get the lines so straight on the border of that picture?" The other student replies, "You've got to mark off the edge of the border with a ruler. Here, let me show you," and a mini tutorial begins.

Of course, like any class, there are moments that are less than perfect. A student is trying to score three-pointers ten feet away from the trash can with wadded-up balls of paper. Another student wanders over to a friend's worktable and starts to talk about last night's Red Sox game. The school secretary booms over the loudspeaker announcing that because of the wind chill we will have yet another day of indoor recess, and a collective groan ripples through the room, distracting everyone for a few moments.

However, these disruptions are the exceptions, not the norm. There is a sense of purpose and excitement that comes from the most fundamental aspect of the students' work: they have power and control of their learning because they themselves chose the topics they are studying. They are invested in the work because it is *their* work.

These children are also preparing for life in the information age. With the advent of the Internet and the world's ever-growing body of knowledge, schools must make a fundamental shift away from having students memorize information to teaching students how to process and synthesize information. Students need to be able to read various texts, see possibly disparate facts about a topic, and discern what that means. ("Mr. Anderson . . . I don't get it. One book says that there is only life on Earth in our solar system, but I read on the Internet last night that some scientists think there might be life on some moon near Jupiter. Which one is right?") A quote attributed to Eric Hoffer hangs from the entrance of Flanders Elementary School (where Andy and I taught together); it sums up the difference perfectly: "In times of change, learners will inherit the Earth, while the learned will find themselves beautifully equipped to deal with a world that no longer exists."

For years, the Fortune 500 companies have agreed. There is clearly a disparity between what the "real world" wants from the educational community and what we have been delivering. As you look at the table below, notice that skills of cooperation and problem solving rank far above the skills of "traditional" schoolwork (reading, writing, and computation). Ironically, much of the standards movement of the past ten or so years has been in direct contrast to these demands. The high-stakes tests of today often focus on the most basic of skills (such as memory, formulaic writing, and basic reading comprehension) instead of the skills that are most important.

Skills Desired by Fortune 500 Companies (in order of importance)

1. Teamwork
2. Problem solving
3. Interpersonal skills
4. Oral communications
5. Listening
6. Personal/career development
7. Creative thinking
8. Leadership
9. Goal setting/motivation
10. Writing
11. Organizational effectiveness
12. Computation
13. Reading

From *Creativity in Action*, Creative Education Foundation, 1990

This isn't easy teaching, however. Teachers are overwhelmed with state and national test standards and students who are more and more difficult to manage behaviorally. So, how does a teacher structure this independent work? How can twenty different students, all at different developmental and academic levels, study twenty different topics, yet still work on common objectives? How should a classroom be structured and organized? How is a community of learners brought together? How does the teacher keep track of everything that's going on and still teach the required curricula? My first attempt at all of this was less than perfect.

A First Attempt

My first year of teaching was a good one. I taught at Flanders Elementary School in East Lyme, Connecticut—a dynamic environment with a supportive principal and collegial staff. I had done a reasonably good job of covering the curriculum. I had built a strong community of students in the classroom who worked well together and enjoyed learning. Both students and parents had given me positive feedback. However, as the end of my first year approached, I felt like something was missing.

Inspiration struck when I chose to read *The Hobbit* out loud to the class. There were several children who absolutely loved the story, and Justin, a particularly gifted student, wanted to try reading *The Lord of the Rings*. I knew that he could, and I thought it would be a wonderful way for him to challenge himself and stretch his already advanced reading abilities. I wanted to give him class time to work on this reading project. I realized that other kids would probably like to design a challenging project for themselves. Having just graduated from college, where I had designed several independent studies, the idea of such studies in a classroom didn't seem like much of a stretch. After all, when I reflected back on my favorite college classes, I realized that all of them involved some sort of elective project. So, I challenged my fourth graders to select an independent challenging project that they wanted to take on. I suggested that they tackle a long and challenging reading project like Justin's, a long writing project, or even an independent research project. First-year-teacher-like, I thought of the idea in the morning, and we started work that afternoon. I didn't stop to think about the kind of preparation and support that it would take to manage twenty-five different independent studies with a group of nine- and ten-year-olds.

The kids were excited, and many of them chose to try independent research projects. I remember quite a few of those first topics: dogs, airplanes, the human brain, baseball, and the effects of cigarette smoking among them. Soon, the class was a busy, happy mess of students looking up information, drawing posters, building models, and writing skits. There were also some challenging days when everyone seemed to lose their motivation all at once or everyone had a problem, and I felt like it would take five more of me to help everyone. Somehow, we managed to get through several weeks of researching, writing, reading, project making, and presenting.

I was astounded by some of the presentations, pleased by others, mildly discouraged by some, and downright disappointed with a few. Overall, students enjoyed the work, and I realized I had a lot to learn about structuring independent research with children.

Here are some of my reflections about the whole process after that first attempt:

- I saw more energy and passion for learning in my students during our independent project work than I saw at any other point in the year.
- Several children pushed themselves to accomplish things far beyond what I ever could have chosen for them.
- Students were interested in what others were learning, and as a result learned a lot about one another's topics.
- I found myself engaged with learners as a coach: pushing here, prodding there, giving advice, and making suggestions to students who were eager for help.
- Those "teachable moments," where I was able to pull the class together for a whole-class lesson on writing in paragraphs or constructing a high-quality project, were frequent and exciting.
- I had not adequately planned for this work, and therefore, students were not nearly as clear about expectations for their work as they should have been.
- Also because I hadn't planned well, the students' work did not always fit into the fourth-grade curriculum set by the district.
- I hadn't pre-thought specific learning goals and outcomes for students, so I didn't have a consistent way of assessing their work.

- At times, the room was a complete and utter wreck, with paint spilled on the floor, newspapers falling out of cabinets, and books thrown carelessly on tables.
- I sensed great potential in this process but knew it needed refinement.

Two years later, Andy Dousis joined our staff and we began to talk about independent research. He had just finished his student teaching at The Integrated Charter School in Norwich, Connecticut. This school made a habit of children's conducting their own inquiries, so from the start, he had also worked with students researching in his classroom.

Each year, with more work and experience, attempts, failures, and successes, this process became more refined and polished. Collaborations with other colleagues furthered this work and helped show the applicability of independent research to many different grade levels and curricular areas. I eventually moved to New Hampshire and began teaching at Dondero Elementary School in Portsmouth. As Andy and I worked with new people and continued to share our learning, we became more convinced that we needed to share it with others as well. This book is an attempt to detail these experimentations and strategies for other teachers who are interested in bringing the wonder and joy of independent research to their classrooms.

Andy and I couldn't help but notice how writing this book mirrored many aspects of the research process. Like our students, we embarked together on an inquiry process that led us to a deeper understanding of a topic in which we were intensely interested. Our ultimate goal was to share our learning with others, just as our students do with their research projects. It was also very challenging. We struggled with the voice of the book and who should write each chapter. We found that the demands of growing families and other responsibilities made it harder to collaborate. Our learning together took us in unexpected and exciting directions, just as our students experience in our classrooms.

This project required an enormous amount of data collection, reflection, and communication. The inquiry continuously brought up two basic questions. First, "What is the research process?" and second, "How can we share this in a book with other people so they will get the most out of it?" We had to analyze how what we saw teachers, including ourselves, doing related to the research process. We also had to think about where we started and how we got to the point we're at now. An awareness that our development as teachers of the research process happened slowly would be crucial in our portraying of ways other teachers could begin to use this approach.

Most important, our belief that learning is primarily a social event was confirmed. Just as students need to work together and share their thinking, we worked most effectively on this project when collaborating. Late-night phone calls, week-end visits, and email correspondences were the vehicles that led us to the most provocative insights and powerful learning moments. And we didn't limit our reflection to the two of us. We connected with our immediate colleagues and carried our thoughts elsewhere, initiating discussions that would deepen our understanding of inquiry. The professional and personal growth the two of us experienced as a result of the research process is immeasurable. There simply is no better way to learn and grow within our profession than to work with other teachers.

Because teaching is so complex, and the possibilities of this particular model of teaching are so varied, this book is merely a starting point. Every year, the research process develops and changes in our classrooms as we take what we have learned and build on it. We hope that you take what we have to offer and try it out, producing a love for learning and sharing that your students will carry with them the rest of their lives.

2

A Research-Ready Classroom

It seems I can't go more than a year or two without changing classrooms. Due to changes in grade levels that I've taught, school reorganizations, and a change in jobs, I've had seven different classrooms in twelve years. I don't mind all of the moving, though, because it helps keep me fresh, eliminates clutter that's accumulating, and gives me a chance to design a new classroom.

On a hot late-August day in the mid-1990s, I was putting the finishing touches on a new classroom (my third). It was not a traditional fifth-grade room with rows of desks and a prominent teacher's desk placed imposingly in front of a chalkboard. Tables of various sizes were placed about the room, and a 6′×10′ loft was nestled in a corner. The class library was open and inviting, with mums placed on top of bookcases. A large circle area with chairs for twenty-two students and a dry-erase easel took up another corner. The room was open and spacious, with plenty of space to walk about without bumping into furniture. The walls were bare except for one bulletin board with the title "Hopes and Dreams," which waited for the students' first goals of the year. I had just rearranged the tables for the twentieth or so time and was placing a large tropical plant from Home Depot right next to the class library. My principal, Cherry McLaughlin, walked into my room to check in and say hi. She looked around the room and said, "This doesn't look like a classroom. It looks like a place where people come to do work!" I considered that a great compliment. (Later in the year a parent commented with not quite as much enthusiasm that the room reminded her of a waiting room at an airport!)

Often, teachers devote most of their planning time and energy to mastering the subject matter they are teaching, or preparing units and lesson plans, both important aspects of our work. The physical layout of the classroom is neglected as an important teaching component that enhances or impinges upon the learning in the room.

The other commonly neglected consideration is the social layout of the classroom. Each fall I devote significant amounts of time to creating a social climate that encourages risk taking and cooperation. As the year progresses, I continue to spend time and energy maintaining our strong interpersonal structures to ensure that students are safe enough to ask questions, struggle with their learning, and support one another's academic work.

Creating a classroom environment that works is the first step to having successful research, and I have broken this down into three major parts. The first is the actual physical organization of the room. The arrangement of the furniture, the placement of resources and supplies, and the spaces designed to display and store student work all affect the way a class functions. The second is the kind of community of learners that I build and sustain throughout the year. Students who feel safe taking risks and who enjoy the people with whom they work are more productive and energetic learners. The final part is the way new materials and work areas are introduced to students. When children know the resources and supplies that are available to them and have practiced using these resources, they are able to be more responsible and independent learners.

Classroom Organization

Think about the places in your home where you most like to spend time working. What are those places? The garage workshop is one of mine, and the study is another. However, the condition of these two rooms often determines how productive I am there. A dad from my classroom recently gave me twenty white, empty shoe boxes from his shoe store. I reorganized all of the spare parts in my workshop. Light switches and light plates went in one box, and bungee cords in another. All of the joist-hangers left over from last summer's front porch project fit into another box, and spare copper pipe pieces from the heating system I installed with my father-in-law fit into another. Now, when I walk into the garage and flick on the light switch, the neatly stacked and labeled rows of boxes give the room an organized feel.

Right now, the study is a different story. A wall of floor-to-ceiling bookshelves is about the only neat and tidy part of the room. Papers and books lie cluttered and piled, not only over the computer desk but also around it on the floor. Hundreds of photos, organized but not yet put away into albums, wait for Heather, my wife, in huge piles on the floor. An old set of silverware sits in the middle of the room, a reminder of the yard sale we're planning on holding this spring. Random items have found their way into the space: a digital camera, a mug (with an old tea bag still inside), several AOL promotional CDs (why don't I just throw them away?), a felt board with felt animals, and an old empty plastic grocery bag. When I come into this room to work, my stomach sinks.

Our environment affects our moods. This is true not only in our homes, but in our classrooms as well. When a classroom is messy and cluttered, with desks jammed tightly together and teacher boxes of supplies piled high on shelves and counters, students feel anxious, tense, and irritable. A messy and disorganized room creates students who depend on the teacher to find supplies, and they feel frazzled and helpless. A neat, bright, and spacious classroom is inviting and relaxing. When students enter, they feel calmer and less anxious. If the room is organized well, they know where everything is and can be more independent and productive.

An effectively designed and organized classroom is especially important when using the research process. A constructivist classroom requires students to be independent and cooperative. If students will be painting, rehearsing skits, designing multimedia presentations, and constructing papier-mâché models all at once, they had better be independent with supplies and work areas in the classroom. So, let's explore some of the key areas of the classroom to consider while setting up a research-ready environment.

Classroom Library

I want students to read information about their topics independently, so I have built an extensive nonfiction and reference section in my class library. In fact, I now have as many nonfiction and reference books as I do fiction books. I look for texts that are easy to read, have lots of pictures that support the text, and have key elements of nonfiction books, such as glossaries, indexes, caption boxes, charts, and graphs. These books help me structure research lessons that are appropriate to the grade I'm teaching.

When I first began to develop this collection of nonfiction texts, I was disappointed that students weren't using them well. I had books about animals placed together in the library, but they stayed right on the shelf. Even during reading workshop, the books weren't being used. Then I took a mini workshop on effective classroom library design given by Martha Winokur from Tufts University. I learned how to organize books in bins by subject so that students could easily see covers as they searched for books, and how to label bins effectively so that books stayed organized. In the fiction section, Roald Dahl books are in one bin and Lois Lowry books are in another. We have bins for poetry and bins for historical fiction. In the nonfiction section, books are grouped by topic: animals, famous people, geography, nature, sports, and history are just a few. Bold labels hang from the front of each bin so they are easy to find. Now, nonfiction books fly off the shelves during independent reading time, and they are used with ease during research periods.

Figure 2–1. Classroom Library

I would love to steal an idea that Shelley Harwayne talks about in *Lifetime Guarantees*. Her school is creating a computer reference system similar to what most libraries now offer to help network classroom libraries in her school. I have talked with the computer teacher in our school, and she says that it is simple enough to do. With a few teachers and parents willing to put in some time, we could begin to enter our nonfiction libraries into a database that could be searched from any room. A student in my room who wants to learn about whales could find books to use in a first- or fifth-grade classroom down the hall.

Supplies and Materials

Supplies and materials must be organized and easily accessible. Plastic bins with labels on the front make excellent organizers for things like colored pencils, markers, sticky notes, and oil pastels. Piles of papers without shelves or bins quickly become mixed and messy. Trays and shelves make perfect organizers for paper, cardboard, poster board, and so on. Having students create labels for the different storage containers, bins, and shelves that house their class supplies helps them better learn the organization of the room and take some ownership over the supply area.

A year or two ago, our school library ditched the old card-catalog cabinets. I immediately asked if I could have one of them for my classroom. I had seen Beth Furuno, a teacher in East Lyme, Connecticut, use one of these as a supply shelf and wanted to give it a try. Each drawer is the ideal size for items like glue sticks, colored pencils, crayons, and other classroom supplies. The label cards on the front of the drawers are perfect for labeling. Students can reach and keep track of lots of common supplies independently in one small area.

When multiple materials are available to students, it is essential that the materials stay neat and organized, for a messy and cluttered room can be a turnoff to both students and adults. In addition, a well-organized classroom cuts down on the number of exhausting questions that students ask when they need things. "Where are the scissors?" "I need some glue. Where is it?" "Can you help me get some construction paper off of the shelf? I can't reach it." It's hard to focus on students' learning when you spend most of a work period searching for supplies.

High-quality classroom supplies are also essential. Children must have access to scissors that actually cut and staplers that actually staple. Markers should be vibrant and clay moist. It is hard to get excited about your work with low-quality materials. These good supplies need to be available to all students, not just the ones who can afford the brand-new pack of one hundred thin markers each year. I even refuse to let children bring in their own supplies to use unless they are willing to donate them to the classroom collection. Students who don't want to share their personal class supplies can use them at home.

A student who was joining my class in the middle of the year questioned this system, and he was clearly not impressed. I explained that if supplies are in the room, anyone could use them. He asked, "Well, what if I want to let some people use them and not others?" I replied, "That's exactly why we have that system!" Having everyone share supplies not only ensures that everyone has access to materials, but it also ensures a social equity that is vital for the culture of our classroom.

Student Workspaces

The location and arrangement of student seating in the classroom is important for several reasons. Desks or tables closely packed together make the room difficult to navigate. Because students will be carrying projects (often with wet paint or soft clay), they need to move from place to place without turning sideways or walking around lots of tables.

Students should also have a variety of workspaces available. Some students prefer to work sitting at a desk or table, while others would rather recline on a couch or sit on the floor with their back to a wall. Clipboards and cushions can substitute for desks during work periods, giving students working on large projects more room to spread out. This can also leave tables open for group conferences or adults who are assisting students. See Figure 2–2 for some ideas about arranging classroom furniture.

Teacher Workspace

As coordinator and facilitator of learning in the room, I also need a place to work and keep supplies; however, this doesn't mean that a titanic teacher's desk needs to engulf a corner of the room. My second year teaching, I drew a scale drawing of my classroom on graph paper to see how much space my desk was really using. My desk, including the unusable space around it, took up one-eighth of my classroom! It landed in the school's storage closet that afternoon and I haven't had another one since. Now when I need to work, I sit at workspaces with students. I devote a few shelves and a file cabinet to my teacher supplies that are off limits to students. An added bonus to ditching my desk is that I no longer have a space to pile papers and teacher stuff, so my classroom is less cluttered. The scale drawing in Figure 2–2 is what my classroom looked like once it was rearranged.

Whole-Class Instruction Spaces

My first few years teaching, I often conducted lessons from the front of the room with students sitting at desks and tables. I found this arrangement frustrating. They fiddled with things constantly and often had to twist their bodies to see me at the board or the overhead. Since they were often looking at each other, there tended to be lots of side conversations while I was teaching. When I first began exploring the Responsive Classroom and conducting morning meetings, I found that the circle area we used for morning meetings also worked as an effective teaching space. Now everyone can see everyone else, so children are more comfortable and respectful. We are equidistant from each other, which creates a more collaborative feel. We all have equal voice in a circle. An easel with a chart pad works well for my teacher writing space.

Although I designed this circle area specifically for whole-group instruction, it is still used during work periods. Kids enjoy stretching out on the floor in the circle area when they need to spread their work out.

It is especially effective to have several whole-class instruction spaces in various parts of the room so that students don't spend all day in the same place. Though our circle area is the main instructional space, we also use the tables at the back of the classroom or the couch area when we need a change of scenery. Moving to a new spot in the room for sharing, partner chats, or other components of a lesson helps keep students fresh and focused.

Whole-class instruction spaces can also double as presentation spaces when children are ready to share their learning. Another consideration for a presenta-

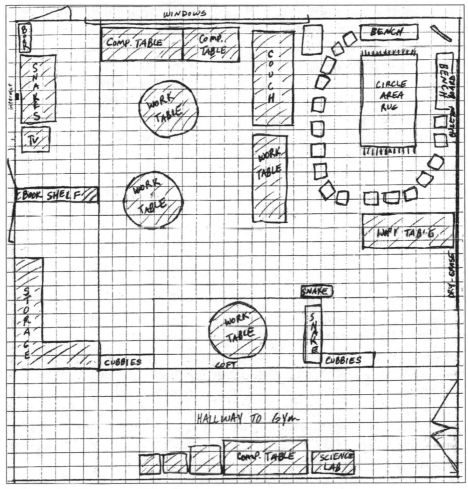

Figure 2–2. Diagram of Classroom Space

tion area is making sure that it is easy to hook up a TV, VCR, DVD, and computer workstation. When students are in the "teacher's spot" next to the easel with posters, charts, and models, and the audience is gathered around in the regular instruction seats, students get to see each other as teachers.

Display Spaces

Andy's classroom used to be a wreck. Though he had a clear system for organizing supplies, he didn't have many appropriate places for in-process and finished projects. Dioramas cluttered bookcases, paintings littered counters and tables, and clay models got lost under piles of posters. During research the room became too messy and cluttered, and the room was hard to navigate. Then Marlynn Clayton, one of the founders of the Northeast Foundation for Children, visited his classroom and gave him a metaphoric "dope slap." She said, "Clean this room up! You need to get rid of this clutter and organize your space. Get up some shelves and clean off these tables!" The mess he had justified as a necessary by-product of constructivist teaching (he was even a little proud of the mess: it showed how child-centered the room was) actually had a negative impact on the tone of the classroom.

Marlynn did more than just point out the messiness of the room. She took a few minutes to coach him in classroom design. She began walking slowly around the classroom. "Andy, take a look at this space here," she began, pointing to a table of clay models and science supplies. "If you add three shelves to this wall above the table, all of your clay models and 3-D projects could go on the shelves, and your table would be free for the science supplies." She walked to another part of the room, where a student had displayed various posters and pictures of ants on their wall space. Several of the pieces were crooked and overlapping. Marlynn started pulling the pieces of work off the wall. "Take a look at this," she said as she began rearranging them on the space. She straightened a few pieces and placed them together in an attractive configuration, took a step back, and asked, "What do you think?" He was amazed.

Those two simple suggestions of straightening papers on the wall and adding shelves to store work helped him reorganize his classroom into a neat and orderly work environment. He shared this experience with me and helped me reorganize my room as well. Now, I no longer accept mess and clutter as natural by-products of constructivist teaching. Work is displayed on shelves and bulletin boards in neat and attractive ways. With a little coaching, students can learn to make use of their space in an organized fashion.

When students are in the middle of constructing projects for a presentation, they will need lots of places to put in-progress projects as well as those they have already finished. Once students have given presentations, they will also need places to display their finished work as a way of celebrating their learning. Dioramas, papier-mâché mountains, watercolor paintings, clay models, and posters take up a great deal of space. They are also what make a classroom come alive. One way to organize all of this work is to create wall spaces around the classroom or in the hallways for student work. Each student has their own 2′ × 3′ space to hang information they have gathered and two-dimensional projects they have completed for others to view. Specific lessons on wall-space organization teach children how to keep these areas visually appealing. It can be easy to allow a classroom to get cluttered and messy when students are creating display spaces.

These wall spaces can also get other students and adults in the building excited about research work. It's fun to watch students on the way to art class

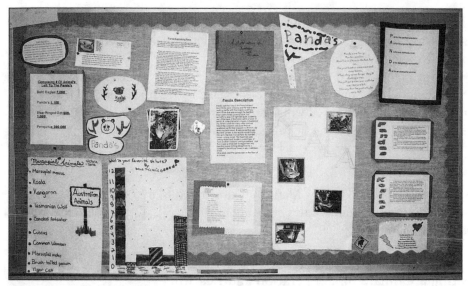

Figure 2–3. Wall Space

pause to look at a poster about Rosa Parks or a crossword puzzle about dinosaurs. Student work neatly displayed all over the classroom gives children a sense of pride and ownership of their room.

Wall spaces have other benefits. At a symposium on reading research, James Hoffman spoke about the impact of a classroom's environmental print on the literacy of the students. He explored what children pay attention to as they look around a classroom, and not surprisingly found that children do not attend to posters and bulletin boards created by teacher preparation companies touting the virtues of grammar, punctuation, and good manners. Instead, children's eyes are most drawn to the print on the walls that comes directly from the work they are doing (charts, class-generated lists, brainstormed ideas, and so on) or to students' actual work. The more we fill our classrooms with authentic pieces of work, the more students pay attention to what's on the walls, and the more time they spend reading environmental print.

Shelves are also important for all of those projects that don't hang neatly on a wall, and for classrooms where display space is hard to come by. A few shelves placed in ideal locations give added space for projects. The shelves should be in a place that is both easy to see and hard to collide with. Shelving outside of the classroom helps show work off to the rest of the school, and shelves in the classroom work well for in-progress work and final project display spaces. Some projects (such as mobiles, lightweight models, or double-sided posters) can be hung from the ceiling or from a clothesline draped across the room. An excellent resource on classroom design is

Side Note: Here are a couple of bonuses to having lots of display space. When students and parents enter the room for the first time at the beginning of the year, and they see lots of empty display spaces waiting for student work (and not lots of prefabricated bulletin boards with cheerful suggestions for how to use semicolons), the message is very clear. This is the students' room, and the students' work is valued. We will share and celebrate our work together. This has a profound effect on the literacy development of students.

Classroom Spaces That Work, by Marlynn Clayton and Mary Beth Forton. Another book that discusses the importance of room organization is *Teaching with the Brain in Mind,* by Eric Jensen.

Creating a Climate of Cooperation and Learning

I remember a fourth-grade class that was particularly easy. I had spent the first month of school teaching them the structures of morning meetings, class meetings, our class discipline system, and other structures in the room. One morning in October, I was late getting out of a meeting. A substitute was in my room to start the day, but I was surprised to see my students engaged in a morning meeting when I entered the room. The substitute was sitting in the back of the class and gave me a sheepish shrug. She whispered to me, "They said they could do this on their own!" Dan had apparently volunteered to lead the morning meeting and the class had agreed. As I was talking with the substitute, Dan had just raised his hand as a signal for quiet, and the other students were raising their hands and directing their attention to him so he could initiate the activity portion of the meeting. He looked at me and said, "Can I keep running this one? This is fun!" I used to joke with colleagues that if I didn't show up for school one day, the students would look around at about lunchtime and say, "Hey! Where's Mr. Anderson?"

Then there was the class that was not so easy. Though they were all wonderful children individually, the class had too many challenges at once to run very smoothly. One student was diagnosed with the early symptoms of bipolar disorder and schizophrenia. Another student couldn't read beyond a first-grade level. Another student had Down's syndrome. Yet another was one of the most ADHD students I have ever met, and he was on no kind of medication at all. There were also four or five students who, for various reasons, struggled with self-control. Thirteen different adults came into my classroom at various times each week, including two full-time paraprofessionals, a speech and language specialist, an occupational therapist, two guidance counselors, and several special education teachers and remedial tutors. This class took every ounce of classroom management skills I had.

Every year a new group of students walks through the classroom door, with their own different personalities and backgrounds. My job is to get the class to work together as a team. This means getting all students ready to ask questions, share with each other, and take risks. Here are some of the strategies that I find most helpful.

Knowing Our Students

Don Graves does an activity with teachers where he has you write down your students' names on a piece of paper. Then he asks you to write a special talent of theirs by their name. Next you are to check off their name if the student knows that you know about their special talent. This powerful exercise helps teachers focus on their children as individuals. When I make personal connections with students, they are more likely to feel valued and connected in the classroom. Knowing something about my students' families and backgrounds will also help me better understand their motivations and needs.

I also need to know my children developmentally. Knowing that second graders cannot read silently (they must whisper) or that fourth graders are often filled with anxiety (note the hair twisting and stomachaches) or that third graders often take on big projects (but struggle with finishing them) helps me plan developmentally appropriate instruction. In fact, as a quick back-to-school activity, I reread a few applicable chapters of *Yardsticks*, by Chip Wood. It outlines developmental characteristics of children in school by age and helps me remember where my students are developmentally as they begin the school year. I also write the names of my class roster in my record-keeping book by age instead of alphabetically. It helps me remember that sometimes the tallest kid in the class is also the youngest and that I need to be realistic about expectations for everyone.

Hopes and Dreams

I begin the year by having my students tell what their academic and social hopes and dreams are for the school year. I want to find out what they are passionate about and what they want to learn during the upcoming year. Students focus on a couple of academic and social goals. For example, they might want to get better at writing, spelling, or math. They might want to learn to solve problems when working with peers or make new friends. I often see students wanting to learn about particular topics, such as rockets, dogs, or ancient Egypt. We discover together their various goals and aspirations, and use this information to tailor our work to their individual dreams. Their work is more purposeful and enthusiastic when it is theirs. (This will be discussed in greater depth later in the book, when I discuss choosing topics for research.) I also have parents fill out a "Hopes and Dreams" sheet about their child for the year. This helps me know what parental expectations are like and gives me a first quick glimpse at the families of my students.

Consistent Rules and Consequences That Make Sense

Students feel most comfortable in an environment where they know what the rules are, and they know these rules will be enforced in a respectful manner. At the beginning of the year, I have my class generate a short list of guidelines for our classroom. We examine our goals for the year and determine how we will all help take care of each other so that our goals can be accomplished. Once we have established the rules, we discuss what will happen when people make mistakes and rules are broken. Students brainstorm consequences that make sense and are fair. When students are a part of the rule-making process and have had the chance to think about consequences, they are more likely to follow the rules and less likely to be argumentative when consequences fall. All of this keeps a classroom running smoothly so that everyone can get work done. For more information about using rules and logical consequences, I highly recommend two books: *Teaching Children to Care* by Ruth Charney and *Rules in School*, by Brady, Forton, Porter, and Wood.

Model and Practice Desired Behaviors

When I first began teaching, this was probably the aspect of classroom management that I neglected the most. I would tell the students to line up at the door, and I couldn't figure out why everyone was pushing and shoving and fighting over who was first. Modeling and practicing desired behaviors before students have to do them on their own lets everyone know what they should do. We establish a common knowledge base about how to carry out routines in the class. This helps students feel safe and relaxed.

For example, if students are going to be able to head down to the library or computer lab on their own to do work, they need to know how that will look and have a chance to practice it first. I lead the whole class on a trip to the library and have them discuss behavior along the way. Which side of the hall should you walk on? What do you do if a friend from another class wants to stop and talk to you? Where can you whisper with a friend and where should you be silent? I have students volunteer to show what it should look and sound like. Then we practice as a class. This kind of work at the beginning of the year gives students a chance to get back into the school mind-set and also gives all students a chance to feel successful (see *The First Six Weeks of School* by Denton and Kriete).

It can be easy to skip through this stage of modeling and practicing, especially when teaching older students. It's common to assume that fifth graders know how to walk down the hall without disrupting others. You might feel like you have too much to do at the beginning of the year without spending three to five minutes discussing how to walk down the hall. Trust me when I say that all of the time spent modeling and practicing the most basic school routines comes back to you twofold later in the year when you don't have to spend time dealing with students who aren't following the rules.

Help Students Know Each Other

Playing games and working cooperatively together in mixed-gender and mixed-friends groups will help all students know each other better. Encouraging and even forcing students to work with those they don't know very well reduces the number and power of cliques in the room and enables everyone to be valued as learners with strengths and unique abilities. Though my students occasionally grumble when I mix up the genders in the room, in the end, they truly appreciate it. Here's what Ahlia, a former student, wrote in a class memories book: "I learned how to work in a group and work with boys. Before I came into your class, I didn't work in groups with boys as much, but when I came into your class you paired up girls with boys and boys with girls (most of the time)."

Another way I get to know my students and to help the students know each other is to designate certain times of the day for class meetings. Beginning the day with a morning meeting is a great way for students to feel safe and welcomed (see Kriete, *The Morning Meeting Book*). Finishing off the day with a quick reflective meeting can give students an opportunity to share their learning from the day. These meetings are times to model and practice appropriate language, empathy, and academic rigor. They are also times to have fun and laugh. Students need to feel connected to each other and the adults in the classroom so that they can take academic risks and feel comfortable making mistakes.

Play

We spend time as a class having fun. We get outside on a warm fall day and play Alaskan Kickball and Elbow Tag. We spend a few minutes every morning playing a short game during our morning meeting. It's easier to take risks while playing a game, and when students can do this, they are more likely to feel comfortable taking academic risks later in the day.

All of these strategies help build a classroom community of caring and responsible students. When students know they are valued for their strengths and gifts and that they are important to a group, they are more able to take risks and learn.

Introducing and Exploring Materials and Work Areas

My first few years teaching, I would get excited about doing a big project with students using paints or clay or papier-mâché, only to be frustrated and disappointed because the materials were hard to use or too distracting for students. Over time, I learned that students need hands-on practice and discovery time with materials before they use them for academic tasks (Charney, Clayton, and Wood 1997). Students have to try things out, discuss and practice how to care for materials and areas, and build a common knowledge base as a class. Students can learn new ways to use materials from each other. Before students begin using things like watercolor paints, I lead an exploration of the paints, letting students practice using them while sharing their discoveries with each other. We become excited about the potentials for using watercolors, and we practice cleaning up as a group so we all know exactly what they should look like after students use them.

In addition to exploring such materials as paints, rulers, and computers, students must practice using areas of the classroom and school that they will need during their research periods. Before they use the library or the computer lab, they are guided through these areas, learning where things are, what they can use, and how to take care of the area. Though this work often takes a considerable amount of time, especially at the beginning of the year, it pays dividends later on. Students are independent and responsible, using materials and areas of the school with minimal adult help. This frees me up during research periods to confer with individuals, conduct minilessons with small groups, and observe the class.

Below are sample lists of materials, resources, and areas specific to research that I might explore and practice with a group of students. While many of these need to be introduced at the beginning of the year, others might be introduced as needed during research time. It is important to note that I often introduce similar materials (like colored pencils, thin and thick markers, and crayons) at once to save time.

Materials

pencils	glue sticks	writing paper
markers	yarn	compass
colored pencils	felt	protractor
glitter	scissors	construction paper
stencils	rulers/meter sticks	elastic bands
crayons	Cray-pas	cardboard/boxes
digital camera	watercolor paints	toothpicks
scanner	Popsicle sticks	video camera

pencil sharpener	modeling clay	audiotape player
computers	hole-punch	clipboard
paper clips	stapler	overhead projector
sticky notes	tape	photocopier
note cards	graph paper	papier-mâché

Research Resources

computer programs	dictionary	VCR, TV, and DVD
Internet sites	nonfiction collection	field trip
encyclopedias	atlas	CD player
CD-ROMs	almanac	thesaurus
magazines	telephone	library computer search

Work Areas

school library	class computers	writing center
computer lab	class display spaces	class library
school office (phone)	math center	tables/desks
media center	sink/counter	art closet
hallway work area	other classrooms	project room

Creating a research-ready classroom is a lot of work. It takes a lot of time, especially at the beginning of the year, to organize a workable classroom space, create a positive classroom community, and systematically introduce key supplies and work areas. The payoffs are unbelievable. The more time I invest in proactive discipline and academic planning, the less time I spend reacting to behaviors and situations that take time away from productive work. The atmosphere of the room is industrious, cooperative, and respectful, and students feel safe enough to set high goals and take academic risks.

Works Cited

Brady, K., M. B. Forton, D. Porter, and C. Wood. 2003. *Rules in School*. Greenfield, MA: Northeast Foundation for Children.

Charney, R. 2002. *Teaching Children to Care*. Greenfield, MA: Northeast Foundation for Children.

Charney, R., M. Clayton, and C. Wood. 1997. *Guidelines for the Responsive Classroom*. Greenfield, MA: Northeast Foundation for Children.

Clayton, M., and M. B. Forton. 2001. *Classroom Spaces That Work*. Greenfield, MA: Northeast Foundation for Children.

Denton, P., and R. Kriete. 2000. *The First Six Weeks of School*. Greenfield, MA: Northeast Foundation for Children.

Harwayne, S. 2000. *Lifetime Guarantees: Toward Ambitious Literacy Teaching*. Portsmouth, NH: Heinemann.

Hoffman, J. V. 2003. "Assessing the Literacy Environment of the Classroom: A Social-Practice Perspective." Lecture, Reading Symposium on Reading Research, University of Wisconsin at Milwaukee, June 13.

Jensen, E. 1998. *Teaching with the Brain in Mind*. Alexandria, VA: ASCD.

Kriete, R. 2002. *The Morning Meeting Book*. Greenfield, MA: Northeast Foundation for Children.

Wood, C. 1997. *Yardsticks: Children in the Classroom Ages 4–14, a Resource for Parents and Teachers*. Greenfield, MA: Northeast Foundation for Children.

www.responsiveclassroom.org

3

Preparing for a Research Unit

The classroom is organized. Students have practiced using the room and many resources and materials. They have practiced working together and have begun forming a cohesive community. I am ready to begin putting together our first research unit. This next section will detail the major considerations of this most important process. As Mike discussed in the first chapter, just diving right into a research unit might be exciting, but it is certainly not the most effective way to structure learning for students. Careful planning can make or break an experience.

Within this phase of preparation, I craft the overall unit, planning major goals, specific objectives, and lessons.

Class Grouping

The first thing to consider is the grouping of students for this unit. Will students work individually or in small groups? Each arrangement has its advantages.

Individual Work

If students work individually, it is easier to assess how much work each student is doing and how much they are learning. It is also easier to work on specific objectives with each child. Dan might need some work with organization, while Sami may want some coaching with public speaking. Jane's goal is to get better at working with other students, and Rico is working on his second language, English. Students who work on their own also have more individual choice. They have more power and control over what topic they study, the skills they practice, and the projects they create to demonstrate their learning. Once students are well practiced at the process of research, this is an ideal form of individuated instruction. Though we have experimented with many different group configurations, Mike and I consider individual work to be the most basic and ideal kind.

Group Work

I first tried this option a few years back as a way of initiating a group of students who were new to the research process. This was a class of third graders who had never done research before, and working together in small groups gave them the chance to learn together and support one another as they went. When students work together, they benefit from the strengths and talents of the group. While one student may be able to read an adult encyclopedia, another may be able to paint a beautiful landscape, while yet another can design a mathematical chart. There are several things to take into account when grouping students for a research project. I prefer to mix it up socially, developmentally, and academically. I make sure to divide up strong groups of friends, mix genders, have high and low readers together, and blend relaxed and challenging personalities.

Students working in groups also have the opportunity to practice social skills such as cooperation, problem solving, and compromise. While working in a group, all students practice the process of researching and putting together a presentation within the safety of a group. When the work and responsibility are shared, everyone can relax and feel successful. These things don't just happen automatically, however. We must teach, model, and practice the skills that children will need in order to work effectively together.

Playing a few group games before the hard work starts gets the group functioning more cohesively. A few of the games that I have found especially conducive to building community are Group Charades, the Human Knot, and Group Juggling. I have picked these up over the years through working with other teachers and taking workshops myself. Here are basic descriptions of these games.

Community-Building Games and Activities

Group Charades
This activity builds teamwork skills and reinforces content.

1. Begin by choosing an overall category for the game. If there is an overall theme to the research unit (outer space, animals, etc.), then that should be the category.
2. Next, split the class up into small groups. Teams of 3–5 students work best. Each team needs to go to a different spot in the classroom.
3. Assign a topic within the overall category that the team must act out as a group. (For example, if the category is weather, the topics might be *tornado*, *hurricane, sunshine, fog,* and *the water cycle*.)
4. The groups get about 3 minutes to prepare a way of acting out their topic. They must act it out silently (no sound effects or talking) and without any

props. The group must act as a whole unit. For example, if the category is animals, and a group has the topic *frog*, then the group of 3–5 students must be one frog. They may be tempted to each hop around like their own frog, but this defeats the teamwork goal of the activity.

5. Finally, each group performs for the class, and the other students try to guess what they are.

The Human Knot

This activity works best for a group of 8–12 students, though I have seen it work with other sizes as well. Players stand in a circle, facing each other. They close their eyes, reach their hands into the middle, and find other hands to hold. Everyone must have one other hand in each of theirs. Once everyone is set, they open their eyes and, without letting go of each other's hands, try to untangle the knot of hands and arms. Students must cooperate for this to work. They have to duck under each other and step over each other. The teacher must set this up well to ensure that everyone knows how to move safely while playing this game.

Group Juggling

For this activity, you will need up to about 15 juggling balls, bean bags, Koosh balls, or other objects that are easy to throw and catch. Begin by standing in a circle. Take a ball and toss it to someone else in the circle. They toss it to someone else, and so on until everyone has had the ball once. The last person throws it back to you. This pattern is used for the rest of the game. The juggling balls will always travel in the same path that was just established. Begin again. Toss the ball to the student you started with. The ball continues on its path until it's about halfway through. Then add another ball, throwing it to the same student. Once that ball has traveled a bit, add in another one. The goal is to see how many balls the class can handle at once before too many are being dropped. As you may imagine, this is challenging and takes modeling and practice before it's played. (What should the tosses look like? What happens when one drops? What's the difference between giggling a little when a ball is dropped and making fun of someone?) In addition to building community and cooperation skills, this game is also a great way to practice memory, focus, and concentration.

For many more games and activities that can help build community and cooperation skills, check out *99 Activities and Greetings* by Melissa Correa-Connolly. It is chock-full of wonderful activities that can enliven any classroom, and a chart at the beginning of the book details what grades they are most appropriate for and which ones are most easily embedded with curricular content.

Class discussions and meetings about group problem solving give kids strategies for working together. After these meetings, we post our list of strategies for solving disputes fairly in the classroom (see sample chart). Many students come into school with few if any strategies for how to work out disputes constructively. It is my responsibility to teach students how to work together productively.

Possible Problem	Possible Solutions
Someone is taking over the group. Other people's ideas aren't being heard.	Everyone takes turns. Do a whip-share so everyone gets to say their ideas. Have a different group leader each day.
Two people each want to do the same thing.	Do "rock, paper, scissors" to decide. Flip a coin. One person just lets the other do it.
Someone isn't working or participating.	Do a whip-share. Make sure to ask them what they think. Give everyone in the group a job.
The group is off task.	Call a group meeting. Make sure everyone knows what they are supposed to be doing.

There are several challenges to consider when children work in groups. Almost always, one student in the group has a hard time contributing as much as others, either because they don't know how to be assertive enough (which gives me a great chance to coach them with this skill) or because they prefer to sit back and have others do the work for them (which usually means they are nervous about taking a social or academic risk in the group). Either way, I make sure to watch groups carefully to assess how different group members are contributing and then do some minilessons with individual groups or the whole class, depending on the need to address this problem.

Billy, a student in one of my first fourth-grade classes, illustrates another challenge to working in groups: students lose some individual control of what they are studying and how they will demonstrate their learning. A bright and energetic learner, Billy had Oppositional Defiant Disorder. Our class was working in teams to research animals that live in communities as part of a science unit. Each group got to choose the animal they wanted to research, and Billy really wanted to study ants. His groupmates all wanted to study dolphins. After a group discussion and vote, Billy lost out on the topic he wanted to study. With arms folded and a red face, he removed himself from the group. It took him a couple of days to be able to let go of his frustration and rejoin the group successfully.

Goals and Objectives

Major Goals

Once the grouping of students has been established, the next thing to consider is, What are the major goals for this unit? Do I want to work on a particular theme or topic of study from my curriculum? Do I want children to get a general idea of how the research process works? Do I want children to practice working cooperatively? There shouldn't be too many major goals for a particular unit; in fact, I rarely have more than three. Especially when I first began trying research with kids, I found I was easily overwhelmed. I needed to focus on just one goal at a time.

The purpose of these major goals is to help focus instruction on a few key ideas. I often choose a social studies theme as the first research theme of the year, since it is easy to find many choices within this subject. My goals are for the children to learn the process of research and explore the social studies theme. I guide children slowly through the process of research through frequent minilessons and small- and whole-group meetings. See the list of goals for examples that one might choose for a particular unit. Although this might look like a long list, remember that I normally focus on only one or two at a time. Once I have decided on the major goals of the unit, I sometimes post them in the room as a display so that we have a constant reminder about the purpose of our work.

Sample Major Goals

- Students will learn how to find information in the library.
- Students will practice working together cooperatively.
- Students will work with different multiple intelligences.
- Students will gain a general understanding of how to put together a research project.
- Students will practice reading and writing nonfiction.
- Students will learn about a famous person.
- Students will write a finished piece of writing.
- Students will gain a general understanding of the American Revolution.
- Students will learn how to find information in the library.
- Students will learn about ecosystems.
- Students will practice setting goals and self-assessing.

27

Specific Objectives

Once I establish the major goals, it is time to figure out which specific social and academic objectives I will include in this unit. These might be items directly out of my curriculum or skills that need practicing for a state or national standardized test. They might be specific social skills with which this particular class needs some practice. These objectives will be the basis of much of my direct instruction during this unit, so I have to be realistic about how much I can get done. Less is usually more. If each skill might take a minilesson plus some practice time, it might make sense to plan three to six specific objectives for each unit.

When I first began doing research with kids, I often got too caught up in the research and would forget about the specific goals. The basic idea here is to integrate curricular objectives or even test-taking objectives into the research unit along with the age-appropriate skills I want children to master. This is how I take care of all of the nitty-gritty learning objectives I am responsible for teaching that I often have a hard time fitting into my writing workshop, reading workshop, or other curricular areas. The following list shows a few possible specific objectives.

Sample Specific Objectives

- Students will practice reading nonfiction texts and explain how they differ from fiction.
- Students will develop and practice a strategy for memorizing information.
- Students will create a time line.
- Students will use body movement in their final presentation.
- Students will plan and conduct a scientific experiment.
- Students will learn how to choose and use an appropriate graphic organizer to organize their notes.
- Students will practice using simple Internet search engines (yahooligans.com and askjeevesforkids.com) to find information.
- Students will develop multiple strategies for solving a dispute within a group.
- Students will practice using the index in a nonfiction text to help them find information.
- Students will practice using the format of multiple-choice questions through giving quizzes in their presentations.
- Students will use a line graph.

For example, our major unit study might be Native Americans. My two major goals might be to have students get some initial experience with research and to learn about Native Americans. My specific objectives might be to teach students how to use an index, to learn the names of three local Native American groups, and to write an expository piece about their individual topic.

Collateral Learning

Though I may plan to teach one or two major goals and one or two specific objectives, it is important to realize how many other skills are being practiced during a research unit. Multiple reading and writing skills, organizational strategies, time management, and social skills are being practiced each day, whether it's planned or not. I call this collateral learning. Sometimes the unplanned teaching moments and the learning kids pick up accidentally are just as important as anything I plan. Through individual coaching sessions, I work with students on specific skills they are practicing on a daily basis, even if they aren't specific skills that I have outlined to teach as part of the unit.

Coordinating with Other Adults

There may be other adults who will assist me with this work. An art or music teacher might help students with projects. Special education teachers and classroom assistants may be in the room to help students with learning disabilities. Parents may come in to help type or take notes. Many different people may be a part of a unit, and it is important to communicate with them before it begins. I try not to take on too much. I often prefer minimal adult help in the room so I don't overwhelm myself with other people.

Parents often ask to volunteer in my class, and I have struggled with this over the years. At times, I have found parents to be an invaluable help, gathering resources that I didn't have time to get or lending a hand in the room so that I have more time for the neediest students. Other times, parents can be a distraction and can generate more work for me. Here are some dos and don'ts that I've developed for myself when inviting parents into the room.

Dos

What are the things that most sap my energy during a research project? Photocopying, stapling, finding websites, typing something for a student who needs assistance, getting books from a library . . . all of the things that I would have a professional assistant do if I were a doctor or lawyer. These are the ideal jobs for parents in my class. I set up a small box on a shelf in my classroom, and any photocopying, laminating, or stapling work goes in the box with a sticky note explaining what needs to be done. When parent volunteers come into the class to help, they know to go straight to the box.

Parents can also be valuable resources in other ways. One year, Mike was struggling to find time to come up with websites that were appropriate for the various research topics his kids had selected. He knew that a dad in his room was computer savvy and was often sending in online articles (and jokes) with his son. Mike called up the dad, gave him the list of topics, and a day later, the dad sent in two appropriate websites for each student in the class.

Don'ts

My first few years teaching, I tried to train parents to confer with students and work with me in the classroom to help teach. My intentions were noble, but the results were poor. I have had a lot of training and experience to become a good teacher, and I shouldn't have assumed that after a few training sessions parents could do what I do. Some parents came in and just focused on their child instead of helping all children. Others used coaching methods that didn't match my goals in the class. I have realized that bringing parents into the room to help with the one-on-one instruction would be like a surgeon bringing me into the operating room to assist with a surgery.

Creating a Time Line

Once I have chosen the grouping of students and have outlined the learning goals and objectives, it is time to put together a time line for the unit. This can range anywhere from a week to several months, depending on the age of my students, the experience they have with research, the particular makeup of students with whom I am working, and the content I am teaching. A group of third graders trying their first research project should get just a few weeks, while an experienced group of sixth graders might take on a two-month study. Though I plan it carefully, I almost never actually stick to the time line I create. An unexpected school assembly or a couple of snow days in the middle of the unit can throw off our timing. Sometimes I discover that I was unrealistic about the amount of work we could get done in a few weeks. This initial time line is a helpful guideline that is almost always adjusted as the process gets under way.

The time line helps me fit in the lessons I want to teach and plan the amount of work time students will need. It also helps me coordinate efforts with other adults. The sample on page 31 is a simple time line for a first attempt at research with a group of fourth graders that I worked with a couple of years ago. The time frame is short (just three weeks) and the major goals are simple: students will get a general understanding of how to put together a research project, and students will learn about animals that live in communities. The specific objectives are also few: reading nonfiction texts, learning some facts about how animals in communities work together, practicing the spelling strategy of memorization, learning how to use Popsicle sticks, and learning how to present information to an audience.

Sample Time Line: A First Attempt
Week One
- Introduce Topic: Animals That Live in Communities: Start a class KWL to find out what students know and what they want to know about animals that live in communities.
- Divide into Groups: play Group Charades and Human Knot.
- Class Lesson: Read nonfiction and take notes.

Week Two
- Groups choose particular animals to study.
- Class Lesson: Decide with the class what information all groups should learn (where animals live, what they eat, how they cooperate within communities, etc.).
- Groups find facts about their animals using books; they record notes on papers and keep in group's folder.
- Class Lesson: Practice memorizing how to spell a hard word. Each group must find a few hard words from their research and develop strategies for memorizing them.

Week Three
- Guided Discovery on Popsicle sticks: Brainstorm ways to use in projects.
- Groups choose two projects to create to share their facts with the class.
- Groups construct the projects.
- Class Lesson: How to present a project to a group.
- Groups present their projects and facts.
- Students and teachers assess work. Verbally debrief: what went well? What will we try to improve next time?

I find that a scope and sequence of the research unit helps me plan more completely. The checklist on page 32 has made this possible. There is so much to remember in the planning stages of a research unit that without some kind of checklist I find myself getting lost. As with the time line, just because I write something down on this research checklist doesn't mean that I'm actually going to do it. It is simply a planning tool that keeps me from forgetting any major steps in the process.

Teacher Research Checklist

Teacher Preparation

- ❑ Prepare the classroom.
- ❑ Choose class grouping.
- ❑ Set major goals.
- ❑ Set specific objectives.
- ❑ Coordinate with other adults.
- ❑ Set a time line for the unit.

Topic Selection

- ❑ Choose overall topic/theme (if any).
- ❑ Brainstorm possible topics.
- ❑ Choose topics.

Questioning

- ❑ Help students focus their research.

Gathering Information

- ❑ Choose and plan research skills to teach.
- ❑ Choose an organizational system.
- ❑ Do research.
- ❑ Set research deadline.

Projects

- ❑ Review goals and objectives.
- ❑ Plant seeds of inspiration.
- ❑ Choose and plan projects.
- ❑ Students work on projects.
- ❑ Model good planning.
- ❑ Coach students.
- ❑ Manage classroom.
- ❑ Begin to discuss presentations.
- ❑ Assess work throughout, through observations, conferences, and work samples.

Presentations and Assessments

- ❑ Plan and design the final assessment tool(s).
- ❑ Choose/teach/model essential presentation skills.
- ❑ Students plan their presentations.
- ❑ Students practice their presentations.
- ❑ Choose audience.
- ❑ Students give their presentations.
- ❑ Teacher and students assess presentations.
- ❑ Students set goals for future projects and presentations.

There is no doubt that the teacher preparation for this kind of teaching is intense. In order for students to be independent and cooperative workers while having some real control over their learning, I must put an incredible structure into place. Isn't it interesting that when people talk about "structure" in the classroom, visions of rows of desks with children sitting still and listening to the teacher often emerge in people's minds? In fact, having a classroom where some students are lying on the floor with books, others are in the computer lab using the Internet, while others are creating a papier-mâché model at a work table takes much more structure than a more traditional model where everyone is doing the same thing at the same time.

So, there it is. One of the most intense parts of the research unit—planning—is complete. Once this extensive setup is in place, it's time for the fun to begin!

Work Cited

Correa-Connolly, M. 2004. *99 Activities and Greetings*. Greenfield, MA: Northeast Foundation for Children.

4

Topic Selection

Shane and I are chatting in class before the day starts. Kids are trickling in from buses, filling out lunch tickets, and meeting in our circle area. "I already know what my next research topic is going to be," states Shane. "Really?" I reply. "We're just starting this one and you're already planning the next one?" "Yep. I figured I'd study Jackie Robinson now, but next year when we learn about American history, I want to learn about the Battle of Gettysburg."

I love it when students have a whole list of possible research topics lined up in their heads. This confirms what I already know. It is not the work itself that is the reason kids get so excited about a research unit. Sure, they love to paint, use the computer, write skits, and present information to their parents and peers, but these things are of secondary importance to them. The fact that they get to choose their topics is what really revs them up.

It is well documented that students are more invested in their learning when they have choices about what and how they learn. (Graves 1983; Charney, Clayton, and Wood 1997). Grace Llewellyn and Amy Silver (2001), in their book called *Guerrilla Learning*, present a powerful insight into the power of learning choices. "In the end, the secret to learning is so simple: Think only about whatever you love. Follow it, do it, dream about it, and it will hit you: Learning was there all the time, happening by itself."

Mike and I were talking about this recently, and he realized that this is true about our own teaching as well. His district recently adopted a math program that everyone must follow. In the past, he loved teaching math. He enjoyed planning the next unit and creating activities that would support the objectives. Though often frustrated by the amount of planning he had to do, he loved having the freedom to teach fractions and decimals and geometry the way he wanted to. Now, every year is like the one before. Sure, he doesn't have nearly the amount of planning to do, but math instruction isn't as fun anymore. Since they've adopted this math program, he's heard more kids complaining about math, due in no small part, I'm sure, to his lack of passion for teaching it.

One summer, I attended a conference at the University of New Hampshire conducted by Jeff Wilhelm, a guru in the field of teaching writing, and he told a story that really drove home the importance of student choice. He talked about a seventh-grade boy who had done a subpar piece of writing. He asked the student why he hadn't put more effort into the piece, knowing full well that this student was capable of better work. The student looked at him and replied, "Well, I didn't choose that topic, you did. That wasn't *my* work." Jeff said that he then remembered a quote from Plato: "Any man who does another man's work is a slave." Jeff let that hang in the air for a moment, and then looked out into the crowd. He finished by asking, "How much of the work your students do is their work, and how much of it is your work? And if they spend most of their day doing your work, how do they feel?"

Since I want students to choose their own topics so that they are working on *their* work, I need to guide them through the process. A substantial amount of time is needed during topic selection for several reasons. I want children to be engaged in work that is real and of the utmost importance to them. I have found that when students take time to thoroughly examine their options, they are more likely to find a suitable topic and become immediately invested in their own learning. Investing time on topic selection can save time and heartache later in the process. A topic that is too broad (sea life, all of World War II, outer space) or too difficult to understand (electrolysis, superconduction) can quickly turn a research project into a frustrating experience. Availability and readability of resources are other considerations. Children need to learn early in their academic careers the importance of investing thinking time in the beginning stages of the research process.

Sparking Interest

At the end of each year, students in our school find out who their teacher will be for the following year, and our whole school has a step-up day. Students travel to their new class to meet their teacher and future classmates. When my next-year students come to visit, I want them thinking about research right away. I have them look at the wall spaces and student work of my current class and ask them to find topics they think are interesting. I then lead a brainstorming session of topics they might like to study when we begin our school year together.

Once a culture of research is established within a classroom and across grade levels, children articulate more specific research-related hopes and dreams. They come into the classroom with research topics in mind and are thinking ahead to their next possible topic. Students who come from other classrooms where research is done enter the room eager to start their first project, adding to the level of excitement in the room. One of the questions I most often hear from new students is "When do we do our first research project?"

I start talking about research on the first day of school and find other times in the subsequent weeks to return to the topic of research in general. It is also a good idea to mention research in parent notices and encourage families to think and talk about it at home. All of this motivates and excites the students. I know it's working when I hear students discussing potential research topics in the hall on the way to lunch or when they first enter the room in the morning.

Establishing a Theme

The first thing I do in this part of the process is decide on the parameters of the topic choices. A social studies or science unit is a structured way to start the year, and it helps keep things a bit simpler. An example is our third-grade whole-class study of Mexico. Students had many choices within this large social studies topic. We began by brainstorming what we already knew about Mexico. Then I did some direct teaching, presenting general important information such as where Mexico is, the language spoken, and some aspects of the culture. I also provided lots of books about Mexico for kids to read. After about a week of immersion in Mexico, we brainstormed possible topics: famous people, famous places, history, culture, and many more.

One year, Mike had his fourth graders choose a New Hampshire animal to study. Studying New Hampshire and animals were both part of the required science and social studies curricula. Students' choices were limited to animals on display at the Squam Lakes Natural Science Center, the site of their first field trip of the year. Another year, in fifth grade, he ran an integrated unit on conflict in American history. After a series of minilectures on various U.S. conflicts such as the Civil Rights Movement and the American Revolution, students chose topics within those conflicts that they found particularly interesting.

However, choices don't have to be connected to an overall theme from science or social studies. Once the research process is internalized and students are ready to be more independent, I allow any topic at all, from China to superheroes, from the effects of cigarette smoking to wolves.

Brainstorming Possibilities

Once a theme is established, we have our first brainstorming session as a class. This first session is short, no more than ten to fifteen minutes. We gather in a circle and whip-share around the circle. One after the other, children share ideas quickly with no discussion. I record the ideas on a large piece of chart paper. I make sure to stop while there are still lots of hands up with more, and a chorus of disappointed "awwws" resounds when I say it's time to finish. This keeps the energy high the next time we begin a session, since kids already have ideas they didn't get to share the first time.

If I think the class may need some additional preparation before this first brainstorming session, I use a few strategies to get everyone ready. I might have everyone turn and chat with a partner for three minutes. Partners list ideas with each other that they might say during the brainstorming session. A variation on the partner chat is the "inside circle, outside circle" share. The class stands in two concentric circles with the inside circle facing the outside circle. Everyone should have a partner. They brainstorm ideas for about thirty seconds, then I have one circle rotate a bit. Kids match up with a new partner and share ideas again. Another way to help kids prepare for brainstorming is to have them do a three-minute quick-write, where they write down as many ideas as they can in three minutes. There are many other ways to help students think ahead about a brainstorming session. I've even had kids prepare for a brainstorming session for homework (see Figure 4–1).

These strategies not only help a class in general, but can also help individual students who need some extra processing time. When leading a brainstorming session, I practice wait time to ensure that slower processors are allowed ample time to contribute. It can be hard not to call on the first hand that is raised all the time. I'll fumble with the eraser or marker in order to extend the wait time. The goal is to have everyone participate and to get lots of ideas on the chart as quickly as possible.

For the next few days, we continue to add to the list. It's amazing how quickly a list of topics grows if worked on a little bit each day. One year I worked with a second- and third-grade class together to generate possible animals they could study. In three twenty-minute sessions we created a list of over two hundred different animals!

Using several class periods over a week to generate the list has a benefit beyond simply generating more ideas. The ideas themselves become richer and

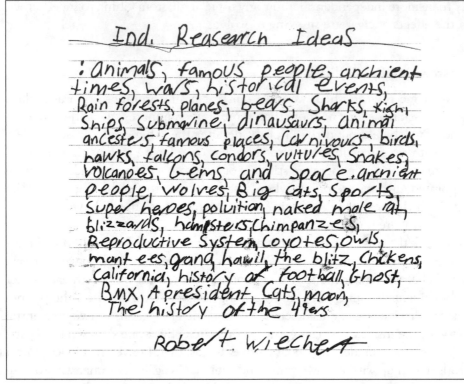

Figure 4–1. This list was created by Robert, a fourth grader, as a homework assignment in preparation for a whole-class brainstorming session. This was an open-ended research unit without an overriding theme for the class. Most of the lists looked like this: varied, interesting, and full!

more diverse when students have time to think more deeply. I remember fourth grader Lisa bounding into class one morning exclaiming, "I thought of an idea for our research topics while I was sleeping last night!"

The chart in Figure 4–2 is a sample brainstorming list from a class of fourth graders about to study outer space. Notice how the ideas are simple and straight-forward at first (planets, the moon, and the sun) but become more varied near the end (Sally Ride, the Crab Nebula, and moon rocks). The longer the brainstorming session lasts, the more interesting the topics become, and this has its advantages and disadvantages. I know that we need to wrap things up when kids start to add items to the list strictly for entertainment purposes. A student once suggested studying the naked mole rat, and this instantly became the hot topic among the boys. A good bellwether for a time to finish a list of famous people is the baseball player Richie *Sexson*. (You've just *got* to love this!)

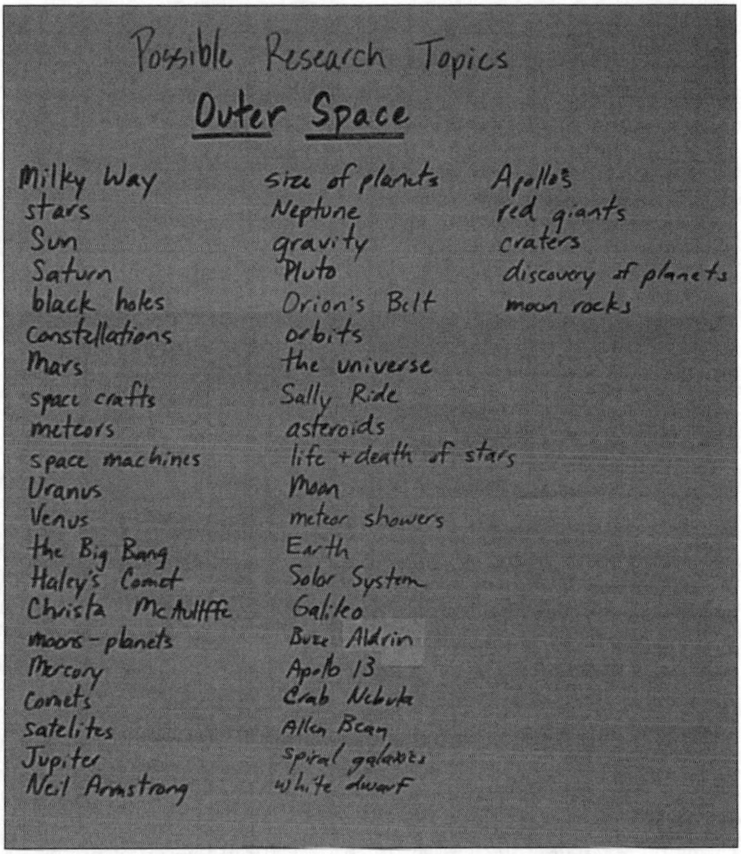

Figure 4–2. This chart took three separate ten-minute blocks to create. This chart then hung in our room for the next few days as students began to choose their own topics.

Choosing a Topic: Establishing a Dialogue

Once the class has generated a sufficient list of topics, it's time for the students to each pick one of their own. I have tried many different ways of organizing this process. One way is simply to sit as a class and have each student raise their hand and state their intended topic. I (or a student) record the list on a chart to post in the room. This is a quick and easy way to pick topics, though if problems arise (someone can't think of an idea or someone chooses a topic that you're not comfortable with), then it can be hard to solve those problems while sitting as a group. Another way is to have everyone write their topic choice on a piece of paper and hand it in at some point during the day. I can then make a chart and unveil it dramatically at the end of the day.

I often have students fill out a topic request form that has them list three to five possible topics with a quick explanation of why they want to study those topics. I then go through the list and comment on ones I feel are most appropriate (according to availability of materials, age appropriateness of topic, and so on). A written dialogue is created that helps establish our relationship during the research process; students have the ideas and the motivation, and I am here to coach, guide, and assist with their learning. When students get these lists back, they can use these thoughts to help them narrow down their selections. Here are a couple of examples taken from a recent class:

John: Grade Four

Possible topics	Why do you want to study this?	Teacher comments
Dogs	I like dogs.	Is there a specific dog you like the most? Do you mean wild or domestic dogs?
Seals	I don't know much about them and would like to.	Last year, children learned a ton about these marine mammals.
New York Yankees	They're my favorite team.	We have a lot of data on the Yankees in our classroom library.
World War II	My grandfather was in this.	Would you use him as a resource?

Paige: Grade Four

Possible topics	Why do you want to study this?	Teacher comments
Nebraska	My family is from there.	I bet they would have a lot of information for you.
Egypt	I'm interested in the pyramids.	Have you considered narrowing your topic down to the pyramids?
Coyotes	We have them living in our woods.	Have you seen any? What do you know about them?
Derek Jeter	He's my favorite player.	You could follow his progress in the newspaper.
Hawaii	I want to go there someday.	Yeah, me too! Why do you want to go?

"Why should I have to write all of this stuff down if I already know what I want to study?" inquired Gaby, a pert and precocious fourth grader. When explaining this process to teachers, I've often heard the same sort of question: "Why spend all of this time having them explain their topic choices? If they know what they want to study and it sounds okay, why not just let them get right to it?"

This dialogue between teacher and student accomplishes a couple of key things. First of all, it establishes the roles of the teacher and student in the process. The student is the one with the ideas, and the teacher is the guide, or coach, who will help the student develop these ideas.

Second, it helps students think more deeply about their topics before they choose them. I once had a student who wanted to study guns because "They're cool." Guns might be an appropriate topic for someone to study if they have a valid reason. Perhaps their father is a hunter or they are interested in learning about the history of guns and how they have changed over time. "They're cool" didn't quite cut it, so I was able to direct this particular student in a different direction.

A third grader in Mike's class one year, Katie, showed a great example of deep thinking around topic-choosing time. Their research theme was community. They had spent several weeks studying various communities in our area to determine the characteristics of communities. Students had interviewed family members about their family community. They talked with their parents about their workplaces and asked questions about how those communities worked. The class also split up into four different groups, and each group went to a local business or organization to explore how those communities function. They collated their data and determined that there were several characteristics that all communities shared: (1) communities are divided up into specific parts or groups, (2) individuals in the community work toward common goals, and (3) each part or group does a specific set of jobs to help the community.

After all this work, students got to choose any community they wanted to study and had to include how their community displayed these three characteristics. Most kids chose things like animals (ants, dolphins, gorillas), a favorite state (Massachusetts, Hawaii), or a favorite sports team (Red Sox, Giants). Katie, who wanted to be a doctor when she grew up, came up to Mike before she filled out her topic request form and said, "I want to study the human body." He replied, "Really? How does that fit with our topic of community?" Katie—who, by the way, would make a fine doctor, but an equally adept lawyer—said, "Well, there are parts to the body and they all help the whole body!" He replied, "I don't know, Katie. Sounds like a bit of a stretch. You'll have to do some major convincing on that one." The next morning, she walked in with the note shown in Figure 4–3.

Unable to argue with this kind of logic, Mike let her proceed with her idea, and she put together a coherent and interesting presentation on the human body,

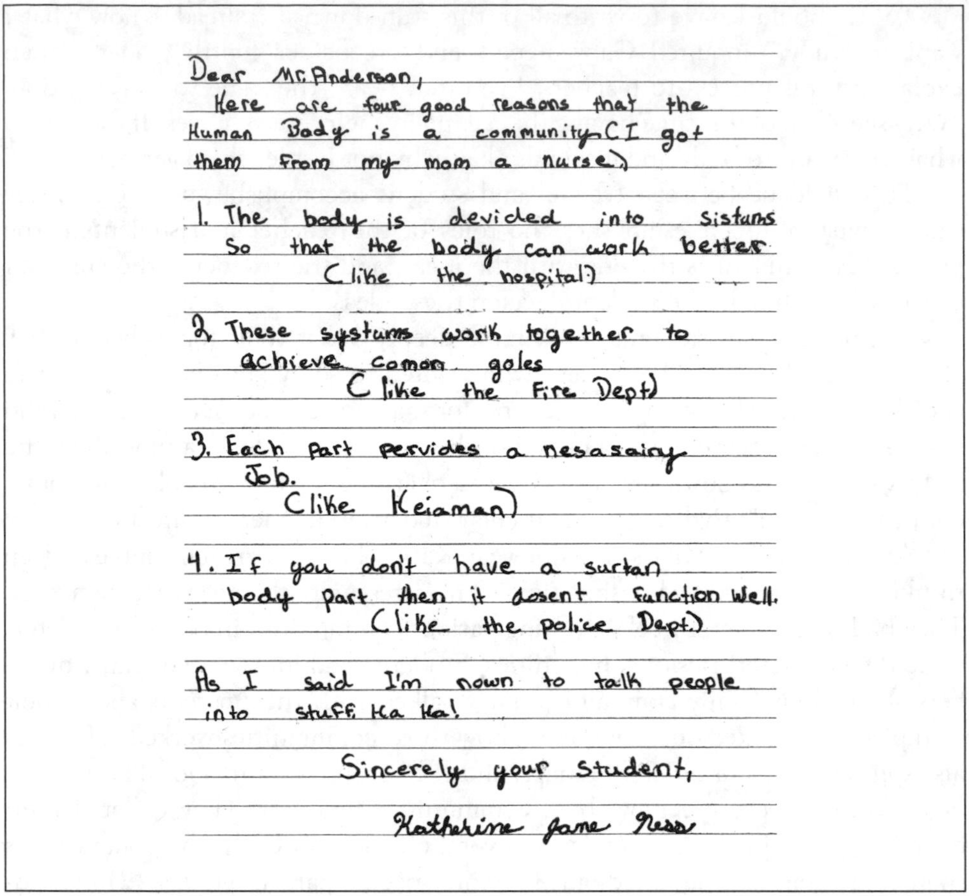

Dear Mr Anderson,
Here are four good reasons that the
Human Body is a community.(I got
them from my mom a nurse.)

1. The body is devided into sistums
   So that the body can work better
              (like the hospital?)

2. These systums work together to
   achieve comon goles
              (like the Fire Dept)

3. Each part pervides a nesasairy
   Job.
         (like Keiaman)

4. If you dont have a surtan
   body part then it dosent function well.
              (like the police Dept)

As I said I'm nown to talk people
into stuff. Ha Ha!

              Sincerely your student,

              Katherine Jane Ness

Figure 4–3. Katie's Note

and clearly outlined in her presentation how the human body was a form of a community.

There have been many other times when students are really set on researching a particular topic and I know it won't work, and I struggle with what to do. I remember one in particular. Katherine wanted to study the Korean War because her grandfather had fought in it. Her grandfather wasn't around, so she would be relying on books for her main information, and I knew that they would be too complicated for her. So, should I let her study the Korean War, knowing that she will learn a powerful lesson about choosing appropriate topics, or should I tell her to find a more appropriate topic so she can learn other research skills more effectively? I opted to let her study the Korean War, and she did indeed learn about the importance of choosing an appropriate topic. Though I helped her as much as I could (do you know how hard it is to explain Communism to a nine-year-old?), she was hopelessly lost through much of the research process. During her presentation, she stated to the class that the next time we did research she would choose an easier topic.

Finally, this dialogue lets students know that I am genuinely interested in their topics. As they learn that I really care about their learning, they tend to open up and take more risks with their learning. They ask more questions and come running to me when they learn something really interesting. This energy is infectious, and soon the whole class is alive and buzzing with students excited about their learning.

Gathering Appropriate Resources

Ensuring that students have a good foundation of resources before they begin their research is a key step of this process. Our research always begins with books, magazines, and other print materials from our classroom and the school library. Though the Internet is an unbelievable tool for our research, it can be overwhelming for many students at the start. It also requires extensive modeling and supervision. (How do we access appropriate sites? How do we determine the accuracy of information? What's the difference between a dot-com and a dot-org, and why does that matter?) So, another requirement of students during this phase of the research process is proving that there are readable resources in the school. It often surprises me what kinds of resources we do and don't have in our school, and I have learned to never assume that our school library will have good, readable texts on a topic. Recently I made that mistake with a fourth grader who wanted to study the Boston Bruins. Hey, we live in hockey country—there must be good books in the library about the local NHL team. He ended up struggling with the Bruins website and a team press guide that he had at home. Both of these resources were beyond his reading level, and his research suffered as a result. I almost made the opposite mistake with a student from the same class a few months later. He wanted to study squirrels, and I told him that there wouldn't be enough resources in our library to support his research. He argued that he could find some, so I sent him to the library to check it out. He returned with four fantastic books all about squirrels and informed me that the librarian had ordered two more from other schools in the district.

Tough Calls

Children often initially choose topics that are overwhelming (such as sea life, outer space, wars, famous athletes). I get to coach them through the process of narrowing down their topic. I have them write down their "too-big topic" at the top of a page and then list smaller subtopics that they might study. For example, a student who wanted to study all sea life might list whales, coral reefs, dolphins, seals, and sharks as subtopics. She would then choose one of these smaller topics to focus on.

There are also times when I really struggle with whether to let a student study a topic at all. One year, four students all wanted to study ancient Egypt. As I read their proposals and met with them in conferences, it became clear that only one of them really wanted to study this topic. The other three were following suit because the first student was such a strong social figure in the room. I ended up redirecting the other three to topics in which they were truly interested. Sometimes I must filter out any silly or inappropriate suggestions. For personal or school climate reasons, topics such as gay rights, evolution, or human reproduction may be off limits.

Harrison posed a tough one for me some time ago in fourth grade. He came up with his topic choice sheet and his number-one choice was the Ku Klux Klan. Knowing the potentially graphic nature of the texts he was likely to encounter, I was hesitant but curious. "Why do you want to study the KKK?" He looked up at me and replied, "Well, you know I'm Jewish, and I heard that the KKK hates Jews just like they hate blacks, and I want to know why they hate people so much." Could there be a more valid reason for studying a topic like this? I called his parents to run the idea by them. They approved the topic, and he went on to learn a lot, teaching his classmates a lot in the process. As it turns out, his topic did cause a bit of a stir in school: he was in the computer room and printed out some pictures of a KKK rally, and the computer teacher was convinced that a student was accessing inappropriate material from the Internet.

Another year, a student wanted to study Lou Gehrig's disease. I couldn't believe it. His mother was in the hospital with Lou Gehrig's disease, and he had never acknowledged this in class. This was another time when I called home to make sure this topic would be okay. His father was surprised but pleased, and eagerly gave his permission. Jim interviewed his mother's doctors, got pamphlets from the hospital when he went to visit her, and did his presentation wearing the hospital scrubs that the doctors had given him. His research work gave him the chance to tell kids in the class what was going on with his mother. It also gave him some power and control over the disease that was stealing his mother from him.

Sometimes requests are just plain weird. We were approaching the end of a fourth- and fifth-grade loop together, and I had set up our last research project as a chance for students to show off their skills as researchers. "Find a topic you really care about and run with it. Get creative," I directed. Justin immediately raised his hand. "I got it, Mr. A. I'm going to study the human arm. Not the hand . . . just from here to here," and he pointed from his wrist to his shoulder.

Now here was a dilemma. I had just challenged them to be creative, but this was pretty wacky. "How are you going to find information about the human arm?"

I wanted to know. "My dad can help. He's got all kinds of stuff about that." His father was a massage therapist, I remembered. Justin was a very bright kid but a bit of a mess. Hair always mussy, shirt always untucked, fly often down, frequently bumping into furniture as he walked through the room, he was the sort of student for whom spelling and handwriting were major problems, but give him a big idea to play with and he was insightful, creative, and brilliant. (He was also a second- or third-degree black belt in tae kwon do, a remarkable pianist, and a creative and talented juggler, all by the age of ten.)

I figured if anyone could pull off a topic like this, it was Justin. With my permission, he proceeded to work with his dad at home to find materials that he could read and understand, and he put together an interesting and engaging presentation. He had the class examining their own arms to feel the different bones. He built a model of an elbow using wood, elastics, and eye screws. It was a great reminder for me of the importance of factoring in knowledge of children and their families when weighing topic choice options.

Other Powerful Topics

Every now and then topics that come along that aren't tough calls but are still unbelievably powerful. One year, I had a student who wanted to research Guatemala. Matt was adopted as a baby from Guatemala and wanted to learn more about his heritage. His adoptive parents later told me that he started asking questions around the dinner table that they had always wanted to discuss but had never found the way to bring up. He wanted to know why his birth parents had put him up for adoption, where he had been born, how many siblings he had, and so much more. In addition to making Guatemalan banana bread and creating a piñata for the class to break open, he shared some of his own family background with the class and we all got to know Matt a lot better.

Another powerful experience happened in Mike's room one year. Robby's older sister was taking a sign language class at the high school and he was interested. He learned about the Gallaudet schools for the deaf, how to finger-spell (and taught the class to finger-spell their names during his presentation), and a bit about the history of American Sign Language. The most exciting part of his presentation was when he introduced his guest speakers. His sister's sign language teacher from the high school had come with two of her deaf students for an interview. One was a huge sophomore from the football team, and the other was a gawky sixteen-year-old girl with the appropriate amount of teenage acne. Both of them were clearly nervous about being in a class of fifth graders, and the fifth graders were just as nervous about having two deaf teenagers in their room. Robby began by asking the teacher a few questions and then questioned the students, using the teacher as the interpreter. Robby then asked his classmates if they had any questions for the guests. Kids glanced around nervously and it took them a while to get going, but once they did, it was amazing. "Can you watch TV?" asked one student. "Can you talk on the phone with friends?" asked another. "What about the doorbell," asked another. "How do you know when someone is at your door?" The questions came fast and furious. Through these questions, the fifth graders learned that both high school students were trying to learn how to speak out loud. Immediately a hand went up: "Can you try and say my name?" asked a fifth grader. Hands shot up everywhere. "Yeah, me too!" the class chorused. The boy was willing to try right away, and with the help of his teacher began saying the names of students in the room, to the delight of the class. The girl was embarrassed and reluctant and the teacher explained that she didn't like to practice in front of other people. She eventually agreed to try and she managed to say, "Ste-ven" slowly and deliberately. The class erupted into applause and the girl blushed and smiled.

After an hour, Mike had to call the session to a close because it was time for lunch. The class would have stayed there a lot longer, and the high school students didn't want to leave either.

These kinds of learning experiences could never be planned; they just have to happen on their own. Giving kids a chance to explore their own interests allows for these kinds of experiences!

Assessment

Even at this initial stage of the research process, I am already assessing student work and behavior. Conferences about students' topic choices give me insights into how they are thinking about their work. Do they choose a topic based on genuine interest or because a friend is studying the same thing? Do they have a lot of different ideas or do they struggle to come up with a few topics that interest them? Each year some students get stuck on one idea for a research topic, and no amount of brainstorming alternatives or writing lists of different ideas will dissuade them. Each class also has a few students who have so many ideas that they can't choose between them. When conferring with students about topic choices, I jot down notes in a three-ring binder for future reference. These notes help me plan whole-class lessons and future goals for students' next research projects.

I also spend a little time each research period observing students. Observation can reveal huge amounts of data about how students solve problems, how they work with others, and how they go about their work. I often jot these observations down in my binder with the conference notes so I can remember what I have seen later on. The notes are often very short: *Jon took five minutes to get any ideas for topics down on his paper* or *Elizabeth always tucks herself away in the same corner of the room when working. Does she like to work alone, or does she feel like no one will work with her?*

Even the simple brainstorming lists and short written pieces that the topic-selection process yields can give me valuable information about students' writing abilities. Especially at the beginning of the year, I learn a lot about how well students can spell, capitalize, and punctuate as well as whether writing is easy or hard for them. I also learn valuable information about students' overall cognitive abilities. Can they think deeply about a topic? Do they branch off of one idea (dogs) into many other possibilities (wolves, dingoes, German shepherds) or are they unable to take it any further?

These initial writing pieces stored away in a student portfolio make good benchmarks for later in the year. I share these pieces of work with parents at conferences to highlight academic growth. At the end of the year, students love looking back at their brainstorming lists from the first month of school to see how much they have grown.

Getting Started!

The day approved topics are presented to the class is always a big one, so I often add a little flair to the event. Once, I posted all of the topics on a chart on the easel and covered it with a sheet. The class assembled on the floor after recess, nearly insane with anticipation. I waited a moment or two and then whipped the sheet off. Students cheered as they saw that they were approved for their choices. Another year students had submitted three choices and rationales for why they wanted to study their topics. I wrote responses and sealed them in envelopes. Everyone opened the envelopes up at once and cheered as most of their choices were approved. Sometimes, it's much more simple. I simply let each student know which of their top choices they can study, and they give me their final decision. Regardless of how it's done, this is a big event, because it signifies the official beginning of the research unit. Students are now falling all over themselves to get started. It is now time to begin the actual research.

Works Cited

Charney, R. S., M. K. Clayton, and C. Wood. 1997. *Guidelines for the Responsive Classroom.* Greenfield, MA: Northeast Foundation for Children.

Graves, D. 1983. *Writing: Teachers and Children at Work.* Portsmouth, NH: Heinemann.

Llewellyn, G., and A. Silver. 2001. *Guerrilla Learning: How to Give Your Kids a Real Education With or Without School.* New York: John Wiley & Sons.

5

Questioning

Children are naturally curious creatures. When my daughters were toddlers, they could spend thirty minutes in the bathtub exploring properties of water with nothing more than a few plastic cups. They poured water from one to the other at various speeds. They watched water as it ran down their arms and off their elbows, then repeated the procedure to watch it again. They watched as soap mixed with water, and they swirled it around to create bubbles. Young children are natural scientists who constantly ask questions and work to answer them. Often by the time children hit the middle elementary grades, a lot of this curiosity has been beaten out of them. They have learned that there are right and wrong answers to questions and that it's a teacher's job to structure their learning for them. So, in this next stage, developing questions for research, we must work to rekindle the curiosity of our students and reawaken their desire to ask and answer their own questions.

I remember the first few times I tried research with nine-year-olds. Once everyone had chosen a topic, I would announce, "Okay, everyone! It's time to take notes! Go to it!" A significant chunk of the class would get out books and stare blankly, unable to start. The other portion of the class plowed right into their topics with little direction or thinking. They scanned the Internet, printing pages and pages of information they couldn't read, and dove right into World Book encyclopedias, furiously copying passages they didn't understand.

After all, developmentally, students in the upper elementary school grades are in the midst of the Piagetian stage of the struggle between industry and inferiority. This energy and enthusiasm is one of the most exciting aspects of teaching children this age. It can also be one of the most frustrating and debilitating attributes for both students and teachers, when quantity and speed win out over organization and quality, and when insecurity and fear of failure lead to feelings of being overwhelmed.

The more I worked with the research process, the more I learned that I needed to help students structure the direction of their research through effective questions. At first, I vaguely encouraged them to "think of some good questions about your topic" and left it at that. Sometimes, I gave them a sheet to list questions, but I gave little instruction on exactly how to think of questions. Many students struggled with this stage, looking up at me with pleading eyes and whining, "I can't think of any questions." It took a while for me to learn how to skillfully direct children toward thoughtful and helpful questions that would drive their research effectively.

Whole-Class General Questions

One class was really struggling with covering the basics in their presentations. Kids would study an animal and neglect to tell where the animal lived. They would study a person and not tell anything about their childhood. I knew that we needed a whole-class structure for covering the basics. This idea worked so well that I have used it with every class since.

At the beginning of the next research unit, we brainstormed all kinds of topics that we might study. Once we had a substantial list on a chart, we began to categorize them. I asked if they saw any topics that fit together. Paige raised her hand and exclaimed, "Yeah! Cheetahs, seals, and polar bears are all animals!" Greg followed with, "And President Bush, Jackie Robinson, and Rosa Parks are all people!" Someone else noted that Hawaii, California, and Paris were all places. I circled topics with different colored markers until we had categorized all of the topics. We came up with a total of five categories: animals, people, places, events, and things.

Next, I put each of these categories at the top of a piece of chart paper and spread them around the room. I divvied the class up into five groups and assigned each to a chart with a marker. Each group had two minutes to list as many questions as they could that would fit in each category. The room erupted in an excited flurry of questions. "How far away is it?" "What are they famous for?" "What do they eat?" "Did they have any children?" "What does it look like?" After two minutes, I rotated the groups and they added to each other's lists. The short time limit kept the groups rolling as they piggybacked on each other's ideas. Once each small group had added ideas to each sheet, we reconvened as a whole group and examined the lists. A few minor additions and adjustments occurred and the class felt good about the lists.

Finally, I passed out a chart to each group and challenged them to make a final draft of the chart that was easy to read and colorful. We hung the charts in the classroom and used them to help formulate questions at the beginning of research units. They provided a great starting point for researchers. If they were studying a place, for example, they could look at the chart and see that they could learn about where it is in the world, who lives there, what it is famous for, how big it is, and what it looks like. Throughout the year, we referred to our charts to make sure that we were getting the basic questions we needed, and I often referred to them during minilessons.

In May, I saw a perfect illustration of just how powerful this activity was. The charts were still up on the wall, but were fading a bit. One of them had flopped down over itself in a corner where the tape had fallen off the wall. We were in the beginning stage of our last research unit of the year, and students were busy generating questions for their new topics. I happened to look over in time to see Alex fully extended on the tips of his toes with a meterstick, pushing the top corner of the poster back up so that he could read it.

Structuring Students' Individual Questions

These charts of whole-class general questions are a great starting point, but in order to get students headed in the right direction, it is critical to guide their individual questions before they begin their note taking. The following are several different ideas for helping students focus their research to keep it manageable and productive. It is important to note that although there are many ideas listed here, I use only one or two per research unit. I have experimented with all of these, and I pick and choose the ones that best seem to fit the group, the age, and the research unit.

KWL

What do you Know? What do you Want to know? What did you Learn? This common format, often used to introduce a new whole-class topic to a group of students, can be an effective way to focus researchers as they begin their fact finding.

Students begin by brainstorming a list of what they know. (I often tell them to list things they *think* they know, since many of them "know" inaccurate information about their topics, or may not be sure that what they know is true.) This serves two purposes. First, students begin thinking about their topic, activating background knowledge. Second, as students think about what they know, they invariably begin wondering about things. ("I know that the Civil War had to do with slavery, but why was there slavery in the first place?")

Once they have listed what they know about a topic, they list things they want to know. This helps focus their research. They refer to their KWL sheets as they gather information to make sure that they are staying focused. They con-

KWL Sheet

What do you **K**now?	What do you **W**ant to know?	What have you **L**earned?

tinue to add to their KWL sheets as they think of new questions as they research. After the research has been finished, students should go back to their KWL sheets and fill in what they learned. Children are often amazed at how much they have learned about their topic in such a short time!

Thinking Aloud

Teachers can model questioning by thinking aloud as they list questions for their own topic or a topic that the whole class is investigating. Using an easel or an overhead projector, the teacher lists questions and writes them down as the students watch. The thinking-aloud teacher may sound like this: "I'm wondering if tornadoes occur everywhere in the world," or "Is it possible for a tornado to really lift up a house like in *The Wizard of Oz?*" I make sure to model what to do if I get stuck: "I can't think of any more questions about tornadoes. Hmmm. Let's see, I know they have really strong winds. Hey! I wonder how fast the winds really are!" While I am doing this, the students record what they see on a clipboard.

It is important for students to debrief after they have watched the think-aloud session. They tell me what they noticed as I was writing down questions. I ask if they have any other strategies for what to do when they get stuck. Recording a list of strategies that hangs on the wall is a way to give students a tool to use as they work on their own questions.

Here is a list of strategies that one class of students came up with:

Think about what you know.
Look in a book for ideas.
Ask a friend.
Leave the list and come back to it.
Think about the basic information you need to teach to the class.
Use the *who, what, where, when,* and *why* questions.
Sometimes you just need to think longer.

Fishbowl: A Process for Modeling Questioning

If children haven't worked on questioning in other areas of their schoolwork, time will need to be spent helping them develop thoughtful questions about their topics. Using a "fishbowl" allows a teacher and student (or small group of students) to model how to generate good questions while the rest of the class sits around them taking notes for a later discussion.

I observed a teacher using this strategy with a class of third graders. The teacher sat with two students (Jake and Marie) on the floor. The students each had a clipboard, a pencil, and their paper for recording questions. The rest of the class was gathered around (looking into the fishbowl) with their own writing materials, ready to record questions and observations during the session.

TEACHER: So, what topics have you chosen to study?

JAKE: The solar system.

MARIE: Zebras.

TEACHER: What are some of the things you think you already know about these topics?

JAKE: I know that there are nine planets in the solar system, and I know all of their names.

TEACHER: Hmmm. That sounds like a solid start. What do you want to know?

JAKE: I don't know. I can't think of anything.

TEACHER: Do you know the order of the planets from the sun?

JAKE: Not quite. I know that Mercury is first, and I know Earth is kind of close.

TEACHER: That might work as a question. How about you, Marie?

MARIE: I know zebras are kind of like striped horses, and I know they live in Africa. I saw them at Busch Gardens when I went with my family last summer.

TEACHER: That should give you a good starting point. What are you wondering about?

MARIE: Well, since I know they are kind of like horses, I'm wondering if they are the same size.

TEACHER (*thinking aloud to the class*): I noticed that Marie's question came out of something she already knew. Since she knew horses and zebras are similar, she wants to find out more about that.

TEACHER (*to Jake*): How are you coming along?

JAKE: Well, I was just thinking that I know that there are nine planets, but I was wondering if there's anything else.

TEACHER: What do you mean, anything else?

JAKE: You know, like comets or asteroids and stuff like that.

TEACHER: What made you think of that?

JAKE: I was watching *Star Wars* last weekend, and Obi-Wan Kenobi hid from a bad guy behind an asteroid.

TEACHER (*thinking aloud to the class*): That's interesting that Jake was able to use something he saw in a movie to help himself out.

The objective of the fishbowl is to have the children observe the questioning process. I think aloud to show students how people in the fishbowl are thinking of their questions. I often focus the audience's attention with a sheet consisting of guiding questions, such as: What did the students do when they thought of a question? How did they come up with questions? What does the teacher do when they get stuck? Can you think of a question they haven't thought of?

The power of the fishbowl is that it allows children to see each other (and themselves) as the ones who have the great strategies. If I were to simply get up in front of the class and share a few strategies for brainstorming questions, it wouldn't be nearly as powerful.

A discussion takes place once the fishbowl participants are done. The observing children should ask questions and make comments based on what they saw and heard. This is an important step, as it further reinforces the process. First, the students hear how to ask questions, then they watch people ask questions, then they debrief and review how the questions were thought of. The repetition is powerful.

Note Cards

Another effective strategy I have used for helping students organize their questions is to have them record their questions on note cards. Each question gets its own note card. When students find the answers, they write the information down on the other side of the note card. When students find interesting facts that don't answer one of their questions, they write them down on blank cards and add them to their pile. This strategy has several benefits. Primarily, it helps students get a sense of how many of their questions they are answering. Later on in the research process, these cards can be organized by subtopic. These organized note cards will help students select projects and organize their presentation.

Although I have introduced this strategy to the whole class, I have found it works particularly well with individual students who struggle with organization. Each year there seems to be one student in my class who drowns in a sea of notes, questions, graphic organizers, and source materials. This system of one question per note card often helps.

Journalistic Formula

A traditional and simple way to structure questioning, the journalistic formula helps students generate a variety of types of questions. It is a good starting point and can ensure that students cover the most basic information about a topic. The teacher can model this with any topic. Providing students with *who, what, where, when,* and *why* sheets can help them get started. A student researching a topic such as the Civil War may come up with the following questions: Who was in the Civil War? What were the causes of the Civil War? When did the Civil War start and end? Where were the most famous battles fought? Why did relatives sometimes fight against one another? The "five W" questions are a good place to start and can lead to different questions.

We recently used this formula as a class and generated lists of questions that fit into each category. For example, if someone's studying a person, there are multiple "*who* questions" to ask. Who was in their family when they were growing up? Did they have any influential people in their lives when they were young? Who were their friends and/or adversaries? Did they have children of their own?

Conferring with Students

A student from a recent fourth-grade class wanted to study baseball. This was a perfect fit. He was a quiet and shy student in the classroom, but a totally different character on the ball field, where he was an animated, take-charge kind of guy. I was hoping that he could transfer some of this energy to his schoolwork with this topic. He tended to miss big chunks of important information when he did research, and this was a topic he knew a lot about. Once the class started writing down questions to guide our research, I called a conference with Mark to see how he was doing.

TEACHER: So, Mark, you must be pretty excited about studying baseball.
MARK: Yup.
TEACHER: So, what are you hoping to learn?
MARK: I want to know about records.
TEACHER: Tell me more about that.
MARK: You know. I want to find out about who hit the most home runs in a season and who had the most RBIs. That kind of thing.
TEACHER: Sounds interesting. What else do you hope to learn?
MARK: I want to find out more about a really great player.
TEACHER: Who do you have in mind?
MARK: Ted Williams. I think he was the best.
TEACHER: I've got some great resources for you about Ted. He's one of my favorites. So you want to learn about statistical records and Ted Williams. What else?
MARK: That's it.
TEACHER: Sounds like a good start. I've got a question for you. Does everyone in the class know as much as you do about baseball?
MARK: (*pauses*) No.
TEACHER: If you didn't know anything about baseball, what else do you think you would need to hear from a presentation on it?
MARK: I guess I'd need to know how to play.

TEACHER: I think that teaching some of the basic rules of the game would really help your audience learn more about baseball. I also think that you'll need to explain some of the baseball terms that you know.

MARK: Like what?

TEACHER: You said that you wanted to know who had the most RBIs in a season. What's an RBI?

MARK: A run batted in.

TEACHER: What other terms might you explain?

MARK: OBP for on-base percentage. Hey! I know—I can make a chart of the terms. It can have the nicknames on one side and the real terms on the other.

TEACHER: I think we will all learn a lot from that poster!

Some learners, like Mark, may only be able to come up with a few questions, and a conference is a great way to get them to broaden their thinking. I try to balance what I think should be in a child's presentation with what they can come up with on their own. I used to push harder with conferences and give students more specific things that they should learn about. (I could have suggested to Mark that he learn about the history of baseball or find out about famous players beyond Ted Williams.) The danger in doing this is that I might take too much control over the work, and students end up researching what I want them know about instead of what they want to know about. This can suck the life right out of a research project.

Here's an example of a different kind of conference. Lisa wanted to research the University of Michigan. She was struggling to come up with questions about this topic, so we sat down for a chat.

TEACHER: So, you're having a hard time thinking of questions, huh?

LISA: Yeah. I just keep getting stuck.

TEACHER: What do you know about the University of Michigan?

LISA: It's big. It's in Michigan. They have lots of sports teams.

TEACHER: That's a start. What do you want to know?

LISA: I don't know.

TEACHER: Do you know anybody who went there?

LISA: My parents both went there.

TEACHER: I didn't know that!

LISA: My mom said it was a cool place and that it would be interesting to study.

TEACHER: Are you interested in studying this?

LISA: I guess not. Maybe I should find something else.

A quick conference is sometimes all it takes to uncover the source of a problem.

Broad and Narrow Questions

Some students struggle with questions that are either too broad or too narrow. Questions that are too broad don't offer a good starting point for research and are overwhelming. (How do you find out the answer to "What are bears like?") Similarly, questions that are too narrow can also be impossible: "Do bears walk just like raccoons?" I often have to help students take questions that are too broad and narrow them down, and I help those with questions that are too narrow to expand on their ideas. The following charts show how this might work.

Broad to Narrow	
Broad Question	**Narrower Questions**
What are bears like?	What do bears eat?
	What colors are bears?
	What are different kinds of bears?
	Where do bears live?

Narrow to Broad	
Narrow Question	**Broader Questions**
Do bears walk just like raccoons?	How do bears walk?
	How are bears like other animals?

Assessment

The questioning phase yields valuable opportunities for assessment. Conferences and observations are again the primary data-collection tools. My note taking often begins to show patterns. The student who struggled with choosing a topic also has a hard time thinking of questions. The child who came up with a really interesting topic is also generating thoughtful and surprisingly deep questions. All of this information helps me plan future lessons and keep track of student learning.

In addition to observing and conferring with students individually, I am now able to assess and monitor students' learning in small groups and through new work samples. I want to know how students organize their work. Can they find their work easily as KWLs, T-charts, and lists of questions are added to their topic selection work, or are they starting to lose papers and get cluttered and messy? As I assess various skills, I plan new lessons based on the needs of the class. One day, five students join me at a round table for a quick lesson on organizing their work, and another day, I pull four students together for a lesson about capitalization. The more the class gets into this work, the more organic my teaching becomes, as strengths and needs of the class begin to shape the daily lessons taught during our research periods. In fact, I often begin to use some of my reading and writing workshop times to reinforce skills that I see students needing during research periods.

A Few Final Words About Questions

Depending on the developmental stage of the learners, the teacher can expect varying degrees of complexity in the questions. Younger learners may only ask questions like "How big can a rhinoceros get?" and "How cold is it in Alaska?" Older researchers may ask more complicated questions such as, "In what ways did Lincoln's assassination affect Reconstruction?" or "How might global warming affect the way we live in Connecticut?" Nevertheless, it is the classroom teacher's responsibility to ensure that the questions are focused and pique the students' interest.

It should also be noted that an emphasis on questioning is placed at the beginning of the research process, but it never really ends. As students answer questions and gather information, they will be led to new questions. (If tornadoes can really occur anywhere in the world, why don't they happen where I live very often? Where do they occur most frequently?) Dealing with new questions also needs to be modeled by the teacher. After a few days of research, I pull the class together and we share the new questions we've come up with. This discussion of questioning helps foster curiosity and the understanding that the learning process is ongoing and dynamic.

The overall goal of the questioning stage is to focus the research. Once students have spent time thinking about their topic, really exploring what they know and what they want to know, they are ready to gather information. And then the questions continue. Though in this chapter I have emphasized how to develop questions at the beginning of the research process, in the next chapter we will show how we continue to ask and use questions as we gather information.

6

Gathering Information

Rebecca runs up to me after recess with pleading eyes. "Can we *please* start getting information now?" Several other students who are gathering in the circle for research time nod in agreement. Micah, a normally subdued student, chimes in, "Yeah! We've been waiting, like, forever!"

Students have spent a week or two choosing topics, brainstorming questions, and organizing their thinking, and they are ready to string me up from the flagpole at the

Figure 6–1. Gathering Information

front of the school. They are *ready* to research. Before I send them diving for the books and computers, there are two things I must plan first: whole-class research skill lessons and the organizational system the class will use as they gather information.

Research Skills to Teach

There are many skills to teach students about the process of gathering information. How to use an index, how to read tables and charts, how to organize notes, and how to write notes using key words are just a few. During reading and writing workshops, the lessons I choose to teach to the whole class are determined by many factors, including the class's research experience, their ages, and the district's curriculum requirements.

At the beginning of the year with a new group of students, research lessons are usually about which resources students will use right away. Especially with a new group of students, I make sure they begin with books or appropriate encyclopedias. Students have normally already found these resources when choosing their topics. (World Book has sets of encyclopedias written at a middle school reading level as well as a fourth-to-fifth-grade reading level. Heinemann has a set of excellent encyclopedias written at the second-to-third-grade reading level. If you have access to a set of encyclopedias like this, they are a perfect starting point for a research project!) First we explore the classroom library, then we branch out to the school library. Once we have collected enough books to begin, we brainstorm a list of other places we can get information, such as magazines, the Internet, videos, and phone interviews. With a group of more experienced researchers, I might move right into more advanced research skills, such as how to tell the difference between articles and advertisements in magazines, how to critically examine the validity of information on a particular website, or how to read historical maps.

Whether the class is just learning about the research process or has been doing research for years, I begin by thinking of just one or two skills that will be most helpful, then teaching a few whole-class lessons on those topics. In any class, there will be a wide range of abilities, so it is important to think about the broad, overall needs of the class, not just of a few struggling or exemplary students. Now is the time to look back at the overall goals and objectives that I planned for this unit and stick to the skills that I determined were most important for the whole class to learn and practice. If a group of students need help in a more basic skill (like using alphabetical order), I pull them aside for a small-group lesson. The same goes for a group of students who might be ready for a more advanced research skill (like conducting an interview over the telephone). I will have time to coach students individually as they need assistance.

Sample Lessons to Teach

How to use resources (books, CD-ROMs, the Internet, etc.)
Using an index
Using a table of contents
Reading graphs, charts, and tables
Using search engines online (Yahooligans, Searchasaurus, etc.)
Finding information in related topics (info about lions in a book on cats)
Note-taking skills
Using computer search system in school library
Conducting a phone interview
Using pictures in nonfiction texts to gather information
Reading maps
Reading time lines
Bibliography skills
Taking notes from a video
Determining who has put information on the Internet and why
Analyzing questions for key words
Organizing data

An example of a coaching session was a conference with Devin about the Battle of Gettysburg. He had chosen this topic for a few reasons. He was really interested in wars, battles, weapons, and history, and his brother had done a research project on the Civil War in my class the year before. He wanted to focus on one part of the Civil War, so I had described a few important aspects of it, and he chose Gettysburg. We were about three days into the research when he asked for a conference.

"So, how's the research going?" I began.

"Okay. I'm not sure that my major categories are working," he replied.

I nodded. "What major categories of information are you focusing on?"

"Well, I want to teach about some of the famous people from the battle, like the generals and stuff. I also want to teach about the weapons they used, the flags from the battle, and uniforms."

"Those are all interesting parts of the battle, but I think you're missing a couple of key components," I said. "A lot of kids in the class don't know much about the Civil War. You'll need to tell them a little background information about the Civil War so they can understand what the battle was about. Also, make sure that you get the basic *who*, *what*, *where*, *when*, and *why* questions answered about the battle. The uniforms, flags, and weapons are interesting, but you need to make sure that you teach the class the basic information as well."

The conference finished with the two of us setting up a chart in his research journal where he could answer the fundamental journalistic questions about the battle. Later that day, I checked back in with him to make sure he was still on track.

Organizational Systems

How often as teachers do we forget to teach children organizational skills? I remember struggling with this myself as a student in school. My teachers emphasized the

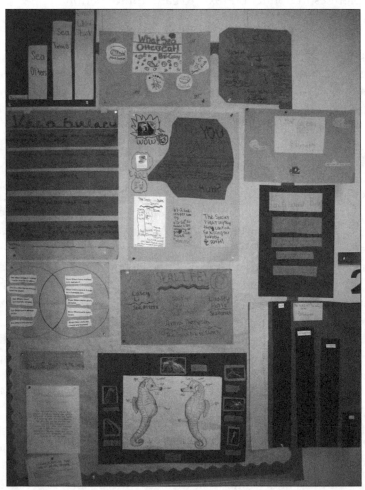

Figure 6–2. Organized Wall Space

importance of organization, but I don't remember ever being taught how to do it, at least nothing beyond the command, "Be organized!" This stage of the research process is an opportune time to teach organizational strategies and systems. An important aspect of all of these organizational strategies is that they must be modeled thoroughly, and children must have plenty of guided practice before they work independently. There are multiple ways of keeping notes and information organized, and there is no one right or best way to do it. Let's explore just a few.

Wall Spaces

In this system, each student is assigned a space in the classroom to organize and display their work. Their space is large enough to have room for notes being collected, pictures, charts, time lines, and other kinds of information. Children begin by creating a colorful title card for their space, and can even post their questions and KWL charts at the beginning of the unit. As students start their research, they post their learning on their wall spaces. The room explodes with questions, notes, sketches, and drafts of possible projects. Periodically, we'll do a museum walk around the room so students can view one another's work. Armed with sticky note pads and pencils, students jot notes to each other about how wall spaces are working. Students often peruse the classroom walls on their own in the morning when they first enter the room. Of course, the challenge here is to keep the spaces neat and organized so that they look exciting and interesting, not cluttered and messy. When done well, research wall spaces are aesthetically pleasing and informative. They offer opportunities for lessons on artistic design, organization, neatness, and many other skills.

Robert was a prolific poster maker, and he usually had a wall space that was overwhelmed by the volume of his work. His spaces became so cluttered that other people had a hard time learning anything about his topic. I suggested that he come up with a system of stacking his posters on top of each other and rotating the order every day. This allowed him to get all of his stuff up there and keep his space neat, and students were constantly flocking to his space to see what information was up on a given day.

Other students have created ways of making their wall spaces more interactive. One year, Amy, a young researcher who was studying dolphins, started posting questions on index cards with the answers underneath. Students could read the question, "Is a dolphin a fish?" and flip the index card up for the answer. This idea was so popular that soon every student in the class was posting index flipcards with questions and answers on their wall spaces.

A third grader named Brian came up with another cool idea one year. He was studying big cats and wanted to survey the class to see which big cat his classmates liked the best, so he posted a survey on his wall space. Kids could go look at his information and the pictures of the cats on his space and then vote for their favorite. They placed their votes in an envelope attached to his wall space. He then presented the results of his survey during his presentation. The key to this was that students couldn't vote blindly. They had to learn something about the cats and then make an informed choice. I liked this so much that during the next round of research projects, each student was required to have at least one inter-active learning experience on their wall space. Some kids did surveys, others made crossword puzzles and word searches, and others had trivia games. When students needed a break from work during the day, they could work on someone's interactive wall space item.

Wall spaces are one of the most powerful ways to organize and display learning, and each year I am amazed at the new ideas students have for using them.

Research Journals

One organizational method that I have particularly enjoyed is keeping a research journal. At the beginning of the year, I go to Barnes and Noble and find simple hardcover journals that I can buy in bulk. When it is time for the first research

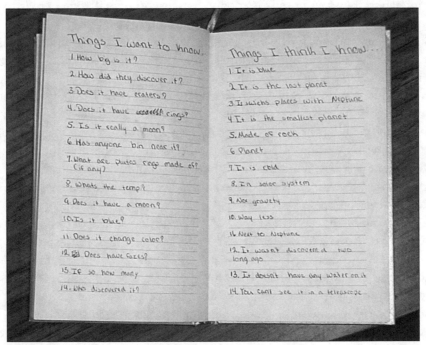

Figure 6–3. Research Journal

project of the year, I make a big deal about how cool and important these journals will be as we research different topics during the year. My students are so excited to get their journals, they just about fall all over each other.

We use the journals to store research work we do all year. We use them for questions and KWL charts. If I am going to have the students fill out any papers for a lesson, I make sure that they can fit into the journals, and we tape or glue them right in. Students initially take all of the notes for their topic in these journals. They also use their journals to take notes during their peers' presentations. At the end of the unit, I make sure their assessment forms also fit into the pages of the journal. In this way, their journal becomes a record of their entire research project, and at the end of the year, they have a record of all of the research they have done. They can also look back at the year and see how much they have grown and learned.

Folders

Another way of warehousing information that students gather is through simple two-pocket folders. Students use them to keep their questions, notes, printouts, project plans, and any other papers together. This system is easy to store and simple to use, and it still affords the opportunity to teach organizational skills.

One of Andy's skilled colleagues, Beth Furuno, has come up with an effective folder system. At the beginning of a unit, she gives her third graders a packet of papers stapled together that they will use as they go: brainstorming sheets, graphic organizers, project idea papers, and so on. These sheets are kept in the right pocket of the folder. The left pocket is reserved for note-taking sheets. This system helps students keep track of their work in a simple and organized way.

Graphic Organizers

There are many graphic organizers that can help students organize their notes as they take them, and can be used in conjunction with wall spaces, research journals, folders, or any other organizational system. Simple numbered note sheets can be color coded later to assist with organization. Journalistic formula sheets (like the one mentioned in the previous chapter) help students organize notes as they take them. Other graphic organizers like T-charts, Venn diagrams, and webs can also be used depending on the research topic, class goals, and individual student needs.

One graphic organizer that I almost always include in a research unit is a checklist for students to help them keep track of where they are in the research process. Once I have the basic plan for the unit, I type up a checklist with the steps the students will follow. It varies slightly, depending on the goals and objectives of the unit. The checklist is especially helpful for students who tend to get lost in a large project. Students keep this checklist in their journal, on their wall space, or in their folder, depending on the organizational system we are using. As they complete a step in the process, they check it off. This is an invaluable tool for me as well for students. When I need to know where the class as a whole is in the process, I simply look at their checklists.

Note Cards

As was mentioned in the previous chapter, sometimes students take notes on cards. Students either take their notes right onto the note cards while researching, or they transfer them onto cards later. Questions go on one side of the card and answers go on the other. Sources can be listed on the back of the card to help build bibliography skills. Later, cards can be color coded or sorted by main idea to help students organize their data in order to build a cohesive and organized presentation. This is especially helpful for students who struggle with feeling overwhelmed when it comes to sorting and organizing information.

Allow Students to Choose Their Preferred Organizational System

Once I have introduced a class to multiple ways to organize information, I allow students to choose the one that works for them. Students are empowered to take charge of their learning and make choices that best fit their learning style. Once the year is well under way, it might be possible to see four or five different organizational systems all up and running at once.

The Roles of the Teacher

A fundamental shift in my role as the teacher occurs during this stage of gathering information. Up to this point in the research process, most of our time spent as a class has been in whole-group or small-group settings. From topic choice through teaching research skills, I have done a lot of work as the "sage on the stage." Once the class enters this next phase, students will do much of their work individually, and my role changes to the "guide on the side." As students engage in the process of going to the library, looking up Internet sites, taking notes from encyclopedias, and possibly conducting phone interviews, I become the coach in the classroom, walking from place to place, answering questions, guiding students through troubles, and offering advice.

Here is the stage where my classroom is truly individuated. I remember a particular scene from a fifth-grade class that illustrates this individuation beautifully. Tim, an extraordinarily successful student, was learning about the Battle of Little

Student Research Checklist

❑ Pick a topic.

❑ List what you know.

❑ List what you want to know.

❑ Gather information.

❑ Organize information.

❑ Confer with peers in your group.

❑ Revise/gather more information.

❑ Plan projects.

❑ Complete projects.

❑ Plan and organize presentation.

❑ Present to class.

❑ Assess presentation.

❑ Set future goals.

❑ Confer with teacher.

Round Top from the Battle of Gettysburg. He was reading a complex text from an adult-level book that I had brought from home. He was enthralled by the story of the twentieth Maine Regiment running out of ammunition, armed only with bayonets, but charging down the hill at Confederate troops nevertheless. The text was a bit too challenging for Tim, so I was coaching him through passages that were very hard. To his right was his friend, Michael, who had Down's syndrome and really struggled with language. Michael was working one-on-one with his paraprofessional assistant, and together they were practicing how to say the parts of an elephant's body using word and picture cards they created together. At the same table were Rebecca and Alyssa, who were studying ancient Egypt and tropical birds, respectively. They were taking notes and helping each other as they went. Here were four completely different kids studying different topics, all reading at different levels, working in the zone that was appropriate for them, each getting the assistance they needed.

There are still some things for me to consider during this stage where students are doing research on their own. How will I make sure to meet with everyone? How do I coach students while they work? Since everyone is working at their own pace, how will I determine when the class is ready to move on to the next stage? We will explore these and other questions throughout the rest of the chapter.

Meet with All Students

When I first began doing research with students, I didn't have a way of making sure that I was getting to everyone on a consistent basis. Instead, I tended to meet most often with those who were either asking for help or getting frustrated and being disruptive. Consequently, students who were quietly frustrated, or those who thought they were on the right track but weren't, didn't get enough of my time and attention.

Certainly, I meet with some students more than others, and I'm okay with that. Some students really don't need as much time and attention here. An occasional check-in every few days might be all they need. However, I find it difficult to even get that quick check-in without some kind of system in place.

I usually have two different ways that I know it's time to confer with a student. First, I have a chart posted in the room so students can sign up for a conference when they need one. This sign-up chart has two columns, one for a student who needs to confer with me, the other for a student who wants to confer with a peer. This system helps in a couple of ways. First of all, it gives me a chance to see who needs the most help and assist them quickly. It also serves an important classroom management purpose. Before I set this system up, I had a hard time moving through the room without being bombarded by questions. "Mr. A, does this look okay?" "Mr. A, what are the first three letters of *brought?*" "Mr.

A, I can't find a computer to use." Now, students aren't allowed to interrupt me when I'm meeting with a student or walking around the room to meet with the next student on the list. Anyone who needs help signs up on the chart. They often solve their own problems before I get to them, so my time is spent with children who are truly stuck

Second, I also need a systematic way of getting to all students periodically, so I make a conference schedule for the week. I meet with four to five students per day so that I get to everyone at least once a week, even if they haven't signed up for a conference.

In addition to checking in with students individually, there are other ways that I can meet with students to assess how they are doing. One way is to have kids get together in small groups to share their progress with one another. I model and practice this format with students extensively, but once it is set up well, I can work my way to the edge of the group and observe their conversations. One group might meet on Monday, another on Tuesday, and so on, so that all of them meet at least once a week. As the year goes on, these groups become more independent, and I play a less-direct role.

Sometimes, I need to get a sense of how the class as a whole is doing. Especially as some students get ready to finish their research, I might call them all together at the beginning or end of a research period, and have the students do a whip-share. They whip around the circle, sharing what stage of the process they are at.

Another method I stole directly from Don Graves' writing status chart. When students come to the circle for a meeting, they are greeted by a chart on the easel that they need to fill out. It might look something like the one on page 70.

Students put their names in the appropriate columns to show their current status. This helps me in several ways. If most students are in the first few columns, I know I may need to give a few extra days for research. If most are in the last few columns, then it's time to move on to the next phase. It also shows me which students might need a little extra attention. They might be too far along too quickly, or they might be moving a little slowly. The chart also helps me plan small-group meetings with students who are all in the same place in the research process.

The Language of Coaching

When I meet with students, I am conscious of the language I use. First and foremost, I want my language to be encouraging, without being too judgmental. Criticism can shut down motivation and frustrate students. When I notice that a student is missing something or has done something poorly, I need to bring it to his attention without a negative or whining tone in my voice. I must also use clear and helpful language.

Writing Status Chart				
I've gathered some information.	I've gathered lots of information.	I've finished gathering information.	I've started working on projects.	I've completed several projects.

Criticism	Instead
These notes are too messy!	I can't read these words. You need to write more neatly.
I'm disappointed in the number of notes you have.	You need to gather more information. Do you need some help finding another book?
You're not working very hard today!	How can I help you refocus?
You're not being very careful with your spelling. You shouldn't make so many mistakes.	Make sure to spell words correctly that you're seeing in the books. Check on these three words.

Praise can also be tricky. I want to give positive feedback about students' work without making blanket judgments about their character. I remember only too well the feelings of resentment that accompanied the easy "Good boy!" praise from my childhood. Praise can also focus the energy of the conversation on the teacher instead of the student. "I like your work. Good job! I'm proud of you!" says implicitly that the student should be working for the teacher's approval. Praise also sends the message that students are working for me instead of themselves. It might seem counterintuitive, but convincing evidence shows that too much praise actually damages and lowers self-esteem (Kohn 1999; Charney, Clayton, and Wood 1998), can discourage problem solving (Stringer and Hurt 1981), and can create children who are dependent on adults to tell them what is good or bad (Kamii 1984).

I want my language to be reflective, specific, and sincere. In lieu of praising work that students are doing, I offer objective feedback that shows specifically what they are doing well. I also encourage them to tell me what they like about their work. My goals are to get children to be better self-evaluators and to encourage them to think for themselves. I also want to reinforce that they are doing *their* work, not mine.

Praise	Instead
In response to a child who has showed you a page of facts they have collected: "Good job!"	"I notice that you have 38 facts that you have gathered in one class period. A lot of your facts look pretty interesting."
In response to a student who has worked for 45 straight minutes on a chart: "I'm so proud of you!"	"You must be so proud of yourself! You worked for 45 straight minutes on that chart. Look at how straight the lines are!"
Do you like the picture I drew? "I love it!"	"Tell me what you like about it." Or "I see that you included a lot of details of this Civil War battle in your picture."

Ask More, Answer Less

One of the most difficult things for me to do when a child asks me a question about their research is to *not* answer. What's wrong with just answering a question, you ask? If my goal is to create students who are independent and thoughtful, I want them to figure things out for themselves whenever possible. If a student comes up and says, "I can't find any more information on pandas," it is tempting to say, "Look in this encyclopedia." (I might also be tempted to answer this question with another question that I already know the answer to: "Have you looked in this encyclopedia?") Instead, I want to encourage this student to problem solve a little. "What have you tried so far?" or "Where else do you think you can look?" or even "Hmmm. What are you going to do next?" All of these questions put the ball back in the student's court. The problem is not mine to solve, it is the student's and is a great learning opportunity. Does this mean that I never respond to a question with a straight answer? No. I just keep trying to make sure that the student is doing the thinking and the problem solving on their work.

Student Questions/Problems	Teacher Responses
What does this map show?	What do you understand about it so far?
Do I have enough notes yet?	Have you answered the questions that you wanted to answer? Do you feel like you have enough information to teach the class?
There's hardly any information on bobcats in this encyclopedia.	Does the article list any other places to look?

Ask Follow-Up Questions

Once students have spent several days doing research, it can be helpful for them to go back to their lists of questions and see if any can be added. If you don't know too much about a topic, it is often hard to ask good questions about it. Now that students know more about their topic, they might be able to come up with deeper, more interesting questions. This can increase the level of intensity of the research.

Sometimes, I will stop the class in the middle of a work period, pass out a note card to each student, and have them record one new question about their topic on the card. They turn to a neighbor and share this new question. I may also have them take five minutes with their neighbor to share some of things they have learned so far. Both of these quick activities help generate conversation about learning and help extend students' thinking about their topics.

Group Follow-Up Questions

If I want students to have more in-depth conversations about their learning, I establish small share circles made up of four to six students. Children take turns verbalizing what they've uncovered about their topic so far. The other children actively listen and in the end attempt to get their classmates to think in deeper and broader terms about their topics. These small groups often form tight bonds and get invested in each other's research. Many times, I've seen students bringing in books and other resources from home to help out their groupmates.

In order for these groups to work, I model and practice this forum before students use it during research times, and I facilitate the groups. My objective is to help students ask meaningful and interesting questions of each other. My other goal is to render myself obsolete in the group, eventually moving off to the side as they become more independent. I have seen successful groups call themselves to order without prompting because a group member needed advice.

Assessment and Record Keeping

My record keeping explodes during this phase of the research process. I walk around the room with my note-taking binder and jot notes to myself about work I see and conversations I have. As I plan each research period, I scan through my notes, finding common themes for whole-class and small-group instruction.

This is usually the first stage of the research process in which I have students begin formally self-assessing their work. They have been informally assessing from the beginning through conference questions. ("So, Jamie, how are you doing at answering your questions?") Now, I begin to have students fill out quick research status surveys, such as the one on page 74.

Assessments like these are useful for a few reasons. They give additional information about how everyone is doing on their research work. More important, they get students to be more reflective about their work. I learn about how students view themselves and their work when I do these quick self-assessments. I remember one student who always found something lacking in her work, even though she was one of the most exemplary students with whom I have ever worked. Ellie would write that she needed more information when she had twice as much as everyone else. In that same class was someone else who did the exact opposite. Andrew was always happy with his work no matter what the quality, and he never thought there was anything that could make it any better, even when the work was sloppy, misspelled, and incomplete. Interestingly enough, both students' self-perceptions were products of home. Ellie's brother was a straight-A senior at Phillips Exeter Academy, a prestigious private secondary school, and she was constantly comparing herself to him. I learned about Andrew when I first saw

Research Status Survey

Topic _____

What is going well with your research right now?

What do you wish was going better?

What will you do next?

him with his mother. She heaped excessive amounts of praise on him regardless of the quality of his work. "Oh, Andrew! That is such a beautiful painting! That is so fantastic! You're such a great artist!" Both students struggled to view their own work objectively, and this was something I worked on a lot with them throughout the year.

These self-assessments also help me gauge when it is time to move on to the next phase of the research process: creating projects. As students show they have obtained a solid foundation of knowledge about their topic, I know it is time to transition to the project phase.

Transition to Projects

The information-gathering phase never really ends. Though as a class we might move into the project phase, students will find they need to gather more information as they create their projects. Some students continue to gather information even after the whole research unit is done. In Andy's class, one student had studied the brown recluse spider. The child had created his own little fan club where he dispersed daily tidbits about the ghastly nature of some spiders. One day Andy told the boy that he had a friend who was bitten by a brown recluse spider and almost lost his leg, and his friend had agreed to come visit the classroom when he got a chance. Evan prepared a list of interview questions for the visit. Unfortunately, Andy's friend was not able to come in time for Evan's presentation. Months passed, and Kelly, a Connecticut College student teacher, was now leading the class, when John—a large, fifty-something former pro football player—walked into the classroom unannounced. Kelly was a little surprised when John appeared in the doorway and said he was looking for Andy. After a brief explanation, Kelly knew right away why John was there. She suggested that Evan dig up his interview questions from a few months ago. In minutes the class was circled up on the rug with John sitting before them, ready for his interview with Evan.

Pictures in hand, John answered all of Evan's questions with a mesmerizing tale of his brown recluse encounter. Andy walked in just as the whole-group session concluded. The class went back to their work and Evan and John found a corner of the room to delve even deeper into the inquiry. The next day Evan made a poster of the pictures of the healing progression of the wound on John's ankle. Evan shared the poster with the class, and the poster then went onto the classroom wall where it elicited many more questions from other students, parents, and staff.

This sort of prolonged interest and passion for a topic is one of the greatest benefits of this way of learning. Evan's initial work on brown recluse spiders turned into an ongoing inquiry. He became the resident expert on spiders and kept teaching classmates and visitors throughout the year.

Figure 6–4. Evan's Interview

Works Cited

Charney, R. S., M. K. Clayton, and C. Wood. 1998. *The Responsive Classroom: Advanced Guidelines*. Greenfield, MA: Northeast Foundation for Children.

Kamii, C. 1984. "Viewpoint: Obedience Is Not Enough. *Young Children* 39 (4), 11–14.

Kohn, A. 1999. *Punished by Rewards: The Trouble with Gold Stars, Incentive Plans, A's, Praise, and Other Bribes*. Boston: Houghton Mifflin.

Stringer, B. R., and H. T. Hurt. 1981. "To praise or Not to Praise: Factors to Consider Before Utilizing Praise as a Reinforcing Device in the Classroom Communication Process." Paper presented at the annual meeting of the Southern Speech Communications Association, Austin, TX, April 8–10.

7

Projects

"Yes!" exclaims Chris as he reads the news and announcements chart welcoming students to the room. He turns to other students who are entering the class and still taking off their coats. "Hey, everyone! It says here in the morning letter that we get to start our projects today!"

As students finish their research, it is time to transition to the project phase. This is what students most look forward to. They get to glue, construct, dance, sing, write, color, move, graph, mold, paint, and more. Project work is also an important step developmentally for students in the middle and upper elementary years. Though they certainly learn a lot while asking questions and taking notes, it is the projects that drive the learning home. Students this age learn by *doing* (Wood 1997).

While students might be unbelievably excited about creating projects, teachers can view this stage with a bit more apprehension. This was the part of the process that I struggled with the most initially. Paper fell out of the shelves, glue sticks were left out on tables, kids ran with scissors, paint was spilled into the carpet, and students fought over who got to use the tape next. Just then a parent and the principal would drop by for a visit, and I would be standing in the middle of this mass of chaos and confusion. Over time, I learned to organize the chaos and set children up to be successful and responsible workers so that we could have dancing, gluing, painting, writing, and graphing all going on at once.

The goal of this chapter is to explore how to structure this work so that students are having fun and learning a lot, while at the same time the sanity of the classroom and the teacher are maintained. We will also explore how to hold students to high academic standards. They are doing more than simply making posters; they are practicing academic rigor through careful planning and effective revisions.

Getting Started

Reviewing Goals and Objectives

This part of the process actually began back at the planning stage. Now is the time I check on the overall goals and objectives of the unit to remember how the projects fit in. If one of the objectives is that students will learn how to use a time line, I require them to create one. If a goal is that students use several of the multiple intelligences (Gardner 1983), they will need help understanding the different intelligences and brainstorming possible project ideas in each area. (This is an example of work that would take place later in the year, once students have experienced the research process several times and can function rather independently.) Perhaps there is a particular art supply or technology skill I want students to practice using. I once wanted to teach a fourth-grade class how to use PowerPoint, so that was the only kind of project students could use for their presentation.

Just last year, I had a required project that worked well. It was the last presentation of the year for a group of fourth graders I was taking on to fifth grade. I wanted them to have some experience wrestling with ethical dilemmas, because the fifth-grade social studies curriculum (American history) is loaded with chances for students to think ethically. I thought this would be an interesting warm-up for fifth grade. As their research was winding down, I gave each student a tough question with a planning sheet to help organize their thinking. Shane, who was studying Jackie Robinson, had to struggle with whether fans should be allowed to shout insults and jeers at pro sports events. Elizabeth had to decide if George Washington was still a great American hero even though he owned slaves. My favorite was Morgan's. She had to figure out if it was okay to keep guinea pigs as pets. She came to me with her question in hand and an anguished expression: "No! This isn't fair! I think animals should be free, but I have a guinea pig and I love to have him as a pet! I don't want to be a hypocrite! Aaaaargh!" These questions had to be read and answered at the end of their presentations, and they ended up sparking interesting class discussions.

Getting Students Thinking Ahead

While students are still in the middle of gathering information, I call a quick class meeting. "What kinds of projects are you thinking about to help you teach what you are learning to the class?" I question. It takes students a minute to get going. "I was thinking about drawing a map to show where Colorado is," replies one student. "I want to paint a picture of the fish I'm learning about," says another. Soon, the class is exploding with children exchanging ideas for sharing their work with each other. Students need time to think before working on their projects. This gives them time to plan out some ideas as they research and brings new energy to the research itself. As we near the end of the information-gathering stage, I refer to possible projects with students in conferences and hold several more quick class meetings to generate lists of the possibilities to hang in the room.

A powerful way to share project ideas with students is by showing them examples of past projects. I have a collection of about thirty presentations on video from past years, and I often pull out former students' presentations to share with the class. In addition to showing examples of possible projects, this gives students an idea of how polished presentations look.

One day, we were getting ready to go home when a few former students who were now in middle school popped by for a visit. They hung out and chatted for a few minutes and then moved on to see another teacher. Mason, a current student, walked up to me after they left. "That girl in the red shirt who was just here, is her name Emily?" Surprised, I answered, "Yeah. How do you know Emily?" He replied, "I don't. She studied Walt Disney when she was in fifth grade and she dressed up like Minnie Mouse for her presentation. You showed us her video." I couldn't believe how much he remembered. I *had* shown this class her video. Mason was part of a fourth-grade class that I had taken on from third grade, and I had showed them Emily's video at the beginning of third grade, a year and a half earlier!

A visitor from previous years can also be inspirational. I have former students come back to my class to talk about research. A class is always eager to hear from an older student about projects they have worked on and topics they studied. These guest speakers are often much more inspirational than I could ever be.

Some classes even go and observe other classes that are working on research projects, to see what it looks like. In the picture in Figure 7–1, a group of third-grade students are taking notes as they observe my fourth graders doing research. This strategy pays off for observers and observed alike. How often do kids get to observe other students at work? Outside of school, this sort of thing happens all the time. Kids in Little League watch high school ballplayers finish practice as they wait to take the field. Brownies watch their older sisters in Girl Scouts and see what they will be doing in a few years. I remember as a kid going to a Suzuki strings institute each summer in Ithaca, New York, where I would watch older and more proficient violinists. I saw what I would do in a few years. So as third graders watch older kids, they get excited about the next year and pick up ideas to bring back their own classroom right away.

The fourth graders here get to be models. They have the honor and privilege of showing off their skills. This is a golden opportunity for me to reinforce work habits that we have practiced. "What should the third graders see when they come in this afternoon?" I ask. "We should be really focused," answers one student. "And we should show how we talk with each other about our work and not about last night's soccer game," adds another student, echoing a mantra of mine.

Figure 7–1. Class Observation

Choosing and Planning the Actual Projects

I remember one of the first times I did research with a class. I allowed students to dive right into their project work without any planning. Christine had studied the sun and thought it would be cool to make a huge costume in the shape of the sun that she could wear during her presentation. She spent a week constructing an elaborate cardboard sandwich (like that of someone on a street corner in New York proclaiming that the end of the world is near). She spent hours painting the sun and making sure that it fit her just right. It was really quite impressive. Unfortunately, she hadn't thought about how it would help her teach facts she had learned, and when she got up to give her presentation, she was a beautiful sun, devoid of any real information. This taught me that most students need structure and guidance to connect their learning to their projects.

They also need time to plan, though we should know going in that students at this age will almost always balk at the notion of planning. Their preferred modus operandi is: dive right in and start working. Sketching out a plan before beginning a project is about as natural as waiting until everyone is on the playground and then carefully reviewing the rules of kickball with one another before playing.

There are many ways to help students effectively choose and plan their projects. Sometimes I sit down and talk with them about their projects before they begin. This quick conference can uncover how much thinking students have done and push them to think a little more. Another method is to structure group meetings. Students meet with each other to share ideas. This increases the collaborative spirit of the class and affords me the opportunity to check in and make suggestions. The way I get students thinking carefully about the kinds of projects they will choose varies depending on the time of year, makeup of the class, and specific goals of the research unit.

One of my favorite ways is through teaching them about Howard Gardner's multiple intelligences (1983). I put a list of the intelligences on a chart, and then we come up with famous people and people we know personally who have aptitudes or gifts in those areas. For example, Tiger Woods has great kinesthetic intelligence, our school's music teacher has fantastic musical intelligence, and Steve Irwin (the Crocodile Hunter) has an abundance of natural intelligence. My students love these discussions, and enjoy sharing which intelligences they feel they have. We go on to discuss how people have different strengths and interests, so if we are going to make projects to share with the whole class, we should focus on our own strengths, and also think about the strengths of our audience. If there are some kinesthetically inclined students in our room, we should create physical activities that help those members of our audience learn about our topics. The list on page 82 shows a few projects that fit into different intelligences.

Almost always, I require a plan for each project before students are allowed to begin working. These plans might be detailed drawings or rough sketches. The following chart is an example of one way to help students plan projects. I especially like this one because it makes sure that each project has a specific goal and is focused on a main idea of their research.

Topic: Wolves	
Main Idea	**Project**
1. What they look like	1. Make a 3-D model and a painting
2. Where they live	2. Draw a large map
3. How they communicate	3. Show pictures of facial expressions, and have the class try them
4. They are endangered	4. Have a graph to show numbers and show pamphlet of Adopt-a-Wolf program
5. Other interesting facts	5. Make a poster/chart

Multiple Intelligences

Linguistic Intelligence
poem, picture book, essay, letter, journal, skit, book review, poster

Logical-Mathematical Intelligence
graph, chart, time line, table of information

Visual-Spatial Intelligence
map, model, painting, diorama, drawing

Bodily-Kinesthetic Intelligence
dance, body-movement game/activity, mime

Musical Intelligence
sing a song or rap, play a related piece of music, write a song or rap

Interpersonal Intelligence
conduct an interview, play a group game

Intrapersonal Intelligence
perform a skit/play, role-play, dress up as a character

Natural Intelligence
nature journal, animal/plant identification and classification, observation

Existential Intelligence
ponder deep questions, raise/debate ethical issues

The most important thing I have learned about having kids plan is that they need time. When I used to allow students to start projects right away, it led to sloppy work, poorly designed projects, and a disconnect from the information they had learned. The more I help students plan, the higher the overall quality of their work becomes.

Modeling and Practicing Good Planning

If I am doing research with my students, then I can model good planning for them. I will hold a class lesson for about ten minutes where students simply sit and watch me plan my projects. I think aloud to demonstrate how I come up with ideas. ("I know I want to have a graph to show the different temperatures of each season in Alaska. Hmmm. I wonder which graph would be best. I love doing bar graphs, but I'm not sure those are best for this kind of information. I think a line graph might show this kind of data best.") As I am working and thinking, I engage students by asking them how I am thinking and what they notice about my work.

I also give student researchers some specific planning sheets that help them get organized and ready to work on their projects (see pages 84 and 85). These sheets vary depending on the class and even the student. Once I have introduced several different forms, students can choose the planning sheet that will help them out the most.

Planning and Managing Group Projects

When a team of students works together on a research unit, they have the advantage of many hands making light work and the disadvantage of having to compromise and agree. One team in my class was studying coral reefs as a part of a class study of world ecosystems. There were times when they worked unbelievably well together. When they painted a coral reef scene on the windows of our classroom, they planned how they would divvy up the work and made sure they included all of the information they thought was important. Their work was careful, creative, and collaborative, and their final product was outstanding. For weeks, people came into our classroom to ask about their painting.

Figure 7–2. Group Painting of Coral Reef

Project Planning Sheet

Map (required):

Important information to include:

Time Line (required):

Important information to include:

Project of Your Choice:

Important information to include:

Project of Your Choice:

Important information to include:

Project of Your Choice:

Important information to include:

Project Ideas

Project _____
Sketch:

Project _____
Sketch:

Project _____
Sketch:

Project _____
Sketch:

Figure 7–3. Group Wall Art

Several times they fell apart as a group, arguing over various aspects of the process. For example, they wanted to create a wall of pictures of various creatures that live in the coral reef. Their picture-wall discussion centered on what color matting should be used for the pictures. TJ insisted red would look best, while Macy was positive that yellow was the way to go. I listened to them argue with each other for a while but didn't step in until one of them started ignoring the others and doing what they wanted without the consensus of the group. I had to fight the teacher part of me that wanted to scream, "Aaaahhh! Who cares whether you use yellow or red! You're wasting too much time fighting about this! Flip a coin or something . . . just figure it out!" I knew that if they could solve this on their own, they would be more likely to transfer the problem-solving skills again in another setting (recess, lunch, with a brother at home, or in another group project later in the year). So, I sat them down, let them know that they needed to solve this before they moved on and had them brainstorm a few possible ways of coming to a conclusion. They said they could keep talking or they could try "rock, paper, scissors, shoot." I left them alone for a few minutes, mostly to see if they could solve this alone, partially because I needed a little break from them. When I returned, they were busy matting the pictures, some on red paper and some on yellow. One of them had suggested this compromise and they went with it. Personally, I thought this made for a fantastic final product! Before this compromise, I felt that yellow was the most effective color, but I refrained from sharing this with the group, knowing that my opinion would likely end the discussion. It was more important to me that they solve their problem than come up with what I thought was the most eye-catching final product.

Setting High Expectations for Project Quality

Setting high expectations for project quality is something else that I didn't do when I first began teaching. Students would often produce posters with misspelled words, projects with tape strips clearly visible all over a paper model, and dioramas that were flimsy and unfinished. At first, I dismissed this kind of work as just an example of where kids were developmentally, and I was afraid to push students too hard. I didn't want the projects to become a chore, and I was afraid of taking over the ownership of them.

However, if students are to learn and grow, we must coach. This revelation came to me not in the classroom, but in the swimming pool, where I coached every afternoon. I realized that in the pool, I was always pushing kids to go a little faster and pulling them aside to help them refine their strokes. I never accepted "That's just how I swim," as an excuse for poor technique, yet I was excusing my students for that very reason in the classroom.

There are many ways to set high expectations for finished work. Rubrics can help students focus on such specific attributes of their work as spelling, punctuation, and neatness. (The chapter on assessment will have more about rubrics.) Another way is to model how I think about the quality as I work. Individual coaching also helps students as they work. Over time, a culture of doing careful work is established. Students slow down and pay attention to details, and the overall quality of work is high.

Encouraging Students to Draw on Their Talents

Every year, I have a student or two with some amazing talent that they rarely get to display in school. I've seen students who are gifted piano players, artists, dancers, athletes, and so on. These students can teach others about their special skills by incorporating them into their research projects. Drawing on the talents of individual students broadens the learning for everyone!

Students Should Work at School

It may be tempting during this phase of the research process to allow students to take project work home with them so they can have more time. Some students almost always beg to take their work home. Occasionally, I have allowed this, but I find myself doing so less and less. There are several reasons. The first is that I want to be able to coach students as they work. When they struggle with where to put the tape on their poster or wonder how to make their model look more realistic, I want to be able to guide their learning. If they're at home in their bedroom, I can't do this. Also, once those projects go home, it can be hard for parents, siblings, grandparents, and neighbors not to try to "help." I once had a student bring in a model of a concentration camp that she and her dad had worked on together. It was showroom quality. The wooden structures were beautiful, the painting perfect. I'm sure she learned a lot and had fun working with her dad, but I had no way of telling how much she had done herself.

During one of my first years teaching, I remember we were running out of time for our research work, so I let students take posters home to work on them. Several came back exquisitely done. The handwriting was neat and clean, the matting and spacing were beautiful, and the designs were interesting. It was the best work from these students I had seen all year. At the end of the presentations, their classmates were equally impressed and asked them about their work during the questions and comments portion of the presentations. It soon became clear why their quality was so high. Here are a few of the questions and answers I heard.

"How did you get those lines so straight?"
"Well, my dad did that part because I kept messing up."

"How did you get your drawing to look so realistic?"
"My mom was going to kill me the first time because it wasn't this good, so she made me erase it and start over. Then she showed me to put this line here and add this color to make it look better."

"How did you space it out so well? You filled the whole poster!"
"My mom put all of the cards down on the poster and showed me where to glue them so they would look good."

It was clear from this interchange that while these three students were pretty proud of their posters, their parents had done a lot of the thinking and work. I want my *students* to do the thinking and work!

Instead of allowing students to work more on their projects at home, I offer them the chance to come in before school to do extra work. It's not uncommon near the end of a research unit to have five or six students roll into class an hour early to paint, draw, and practice. These usually turn into fun sessions with small groups that I wish I could do more of during the regular day. A few doughnuts and some orange juice can go a long way toward making these morning sessions fun!

Employing the Expertise of Others

One of our custodians is a sports expert and is often used as a resource when students are learning about baseball. Our art teacher is always willing to share her talents with our class or with an individual researcher who has a particular goal. There are many other adults who can be resources: the librarian, music teacher, physical education teacher, secretaries, principal, other teachers, paraprofessionals, parents. My class gets to learn interesting information and talents from others in the building, and a powerful message is also being learned: everyone has something to share, and learning does not just take place in the classroom.

A Few Words of Wisdom

It is important to constantly reinforce that the purpose of the projects is to teach others about the topics students have studied. When I first began working on this process, I was sometimes disappointed in the projects students chose. There were some projects that just didn't teach much. I remember a student who decided to take a class survey about favorite rides at Disney World. She traveled the room asking everyone what their favorite ride was. She compiled the results and presented them to the class. Unfortunately, this student didn't teach anyone else anything about the rides, so students chose blindly. Many of them had never been to Disney World, so they just picked one at random. While taking a poll and graphing the results might be a valuable activity, the poll itself didn't teach anybody anything about Disney World rides. Sometimes, students get so excited about the prospects of painting or doing papier-mâché that they lose sight of the purpose of the projects, namely to share information they have learned. I need to gently guide students to make appropriate project choices. I usually say, "Explain to me what you are teaching with this project." This helps the students refocus on the ultimate goal of sharing their learning with others.

It is also important to go slowly. Each year, I fight the urge to assume that because I taught something last year, my new class must already know it. ("What do you mean you don't know how to organize a presentation? I worked on this all of last year!") With each new class, I must start simply—limiting choices, taking small steps—until the class has enough experience to be ready for more.

Project-Creation Time

The time when students are actually creating the projects for their presentations is my favorite part of the process. The room is covered in paper, cardboard, painting supplies, toothpicks, clay, glue, and rulers. Projects begin to emerge and go on display: a 3-D model of a World War II fighter jet, a time line about the life of Martin Luther King Jr., a map of Tennessee. The room has a productive hum about it as students immerse themselves in their work and feel productive and excited. Other teachers begin to poke their heads in the door to see what is going on.

In order for all of this to be possible, several preliminary things must happen. Although I have set the classroom up from the beginning of the year so that it is ready for this step of the research process, now is the time to make sure the details are just right.

Classroom Organization

Class Supplies

Students must have access to all of the supplies they will be working with. The supplies need to be neat, organized, easy to reach, age appropriate, and high quality. (I make sure to have good adult-sized scissors for students to use. Have you ever tried to cut anything with those tiny little student ones?) Students also need to have had ample experience and practice with the supplies before they are used for work. I make available only the supplies we have practiced using. If necessary for a particular group, I may limit choices of supplies, and remove a few from the classroom during this time.

Work Areas

My classroom has many clean and open spaces for students to work. I always make sure to have some tables and counters open for painting, clay work, and other messy projects. It is also a good idea to have large spaces on the floor available for students who are constructing huge posters and models. A few out-of-the-way nooks are provided for students who work best on their own with few distractions. Students also need to be able to navigate the room easily. I know my room is getting a bit cluttered if children are bumping into each other or accidentally knocking into one another's projects.

Display Spaces

As students work on projects and eventually finish them up, they will need places to put their work. Display spaces afford students the opportunity to show off their efforts as well as keep work in progress safe. Bulletin boards, wall spaces, bookshelves, and countertops are just a few places for projects. In some classrooms, I have installed shelves around the perimeter of the room.

If each child has a wall space for displaying his work, then I need to do some prep work with him on wall-space design. We might discuss effective use of space, or how to attach work while keeping it safe and without showing gobs of tape. These spaces can be a wonderful way to display work and encourage students to learn about one another's topics.

Teachers' Roles

As students work on various projects, I assume many roles in the classroom. When students work independently, I am the one who holds everything together from behind the scenes. This is the time when other adults walk into my classroom and have a hard time finding me at first. I may be on the floor giving advice or off in a corner having a conference. I might be modeling a skill for a group or simply observing. People stop to gaze in wonder at how independent and self-sufficient my students appear. I have heard from many teachers, "My students could never handle this kind of work." Though often occurring behind the scenes, these various roles that the teacher assumes are what make this part of the process effective.

Modeling

I know that from time to time in my class I explain something to my students and am greeted by "deer in the headlights" eyes. Though the directions made sense to me, they were as clear as mud to the students. I experienced the same thing myself recently as a learner. My father-in-law was teaching me how to do wiring in a room we were adding to our house. He would explain how to wire a particular circuit ("Just jumper the two things into the sister-housing and make a mad-tie to the cow furnace. It's easy!"), and I would be left looking and feeling as dumb as I actually was. For me to better understand what he meant, he had to show me the actual wiring and then I had to do it with him standing there guiding me along. In fact, it took more than once. I needed repeated practice with guidance. Each time we worked together I felt like I understood a little more. This is how modeling works; it gives students a chance to see what they should be doing. They are apprentices gaining practice with a skilled mentor.

I spend a little bit of the project-creation time working on projects of my own for the research project I have been conducting. I position myself near students who I feel may need some extra guidance so I can chat informally with them about how I am thinking as I work. I also work on some projects before or after school and share them with the whole class. Then, I can discuss with everyone what I worked on and struggled with.

Here is a great example of how powerful modeling can be: I was studying tornadoes, and I was trying to create a large bar graph that showed the different levels of the Fujita Scale for measuring wind speeds. I wanted each bar to look like a tornado coming up out of the bottom of the graph. It looked fine when I planned it out on a small piece of graph paper, but when I began drawing it on a large piece of chart paper, the last tornado on the page kept getting too big. It was getting cramped and squished as I attempted to fit it on the paper. I was actually getting quite frustrated by my third or fourth attempt, and students began to try to make

91

me feel better. "Don't worry, Mr. Anderson. It looks fine. We know what it means. You don't have to do another one." I got to respond: "No. When I get up in front of the class to give my presentation, I want this to look just right. I won't feel good about this poster unless it all fits on the page. I'll keep trying."

In the end, students got to see how I solved my problem. More important, I was able to model academic rigor and personal high standards for my work. Many students in the class suddenly began paying attention to how much tape was showing on their poster and the quality of their handwriting.

Coaching for Revision

Just like writing workshop, revision is one of the most important tools for raising the quality of students' work, and just as with their writing, revision is something students are likely to balk at. Going back and making changes is not something that most people relish, and kids in the upper elementary and middle school years find it especially frustrating. This is the tool teachers have for helping students work in their optimal learning zone, that magical place between what they can do on their own and what is beyond their abilities, that place of tension where they are able to struggle through something challenging and learn new skills with coaching and guidance.

I monitor students' progress daily through conferences and quick check-ins. It is important to dispense advice as needed, but not to overdo it. Since each child is working at their individual level, it doesn't make sense to hold everyone to the same standards during the project time. Someone who really struggles with fine motor control may have a project where the lines aren't straight and the tape is showing. A student who is a struggling reader and writer is likely to have a spelling mistake or two. I must assess how much emphasis to place on the final quality of the projects based on my knowledge of the strengths and abilities of each student. Students can work on one or two things at a time, but to expect that everyone will develop projects that look like adults produced them is unreasonable. I must remember to let fourth graders be fourth graders.

By the same token, a good coach is one who pushes students to achieve the best they can. Once, a student approached Andy with a clay model of a shark he had just finished. It was a rough tube of clay that looked like a pinecone with several large tumors. In front, it had two pencil holes for eyes and a cartoon-like smiley face. This student was capable of much better work, and Andy estimated that the model had taken about three minutes to construct.

"Jeff, the shape of this shark doesn't seem quite right. You also told me the other day about how sharks have gills, but I don't see any on your model. I also think that the face looks more like a cartoon shark. This needs more work."

Jeff didn't look happy, but nodded and returned to his workstation. Andy watched to see what he would do. He made a few minor changes and returned about two minutes later. "What do you think now?" he asked. Andy returned the question: "What do you think?" Jeff looked at the shark and said, "I added the gills." Andy replied, "I see that. What are you going to do next?" Jeff replied, "I don't know. It looks okay to me." At this point, Andy was more directive. "Jeff, go get one of the books you used for your research and look up a picture that can help you see all of the details of a shark's body. I know you can create a model that looks realistic." Jeff spent the next thirty minutes looking at the book and making modifications to his model. When he returned, the shark was sleek, well proportioned, and had realistic facial features. Andy asked him what he thought, and Jeff replied, "*This* looks like a shark!"

By not allowing Jeff to get away with a shoddy job, Andy pushed him to create something he was proud of. The suggestion of where to get help was the little nudge he needed to be able to produce better work. In the end, he owned this project because Andy never laid a finger on the clay. Andy also used language that told him specifically what needed work without negative value judgments. ("The shape of this shark doesn't seem quite right" instead of "You haven't worked very hard on this. Why didn't you try harder?") The specific language empowered Jeff. Andy's removing the judging tone from his voice allowed Jeff to focus on the work at hand, not how Andy was feeling about him.

Another example of good coaching involved a student creating a poster about alligators. Tory had worked hard to spell everything correctly, mat text and pictures on different-colored construction paper, and write as neatly as she could. Overall the poster was well done and had taken a lot of time and effort. We were having a conference about her work and to lead things off, I had her list the things that she thought definitely worked well on her poster. She was able to list many ideas: "I really like the color. I got some cool information. I tried to write neatly. The pictures really match my information." I followed up with another question. "If you could change anything about this poster, what would you change?" She thought for a moment and replied, "I don't like how there's all of this blank space on the right side of the poster. It looks like it's not finished, like there should be something else there. I wish I could move the stuff on the poster around, but it will make it look messy to erase all of that stuff and write it over." I suggested that she cut out the parts she wanted, mat them on different-colored paper, and place them on a new posterboard, arranging them the way she wanted before gluing them down. The result was a poster she was much happier about that was clearly an improvement over her first draft. This revision didn't help just Tory. Several other children listened in on our conference and decided to do similar revisions to their own posters. This made Tory feel even better because she had inspired classmates with her own work.

Facilitating Groups

In addition to coaching students individually, I make sure to facilitate groups of students. These groups work together to help each other as they work on their projects. The groups consist of four to seven students and the teacher. I prefer to let the kids do most of the talking. I jump in to help the group along or fill in a hole in the conversation. The following dialogue occurred recently in my classroom during one of these small-group meetings. It's interesting to note that Julie is a student who receives special education services.

> JULIE: I'm researching dolphins, because they're intelligent, and I want to learn more about them. I'm having fun, and I'm making a clay sculpture of a dolphin.

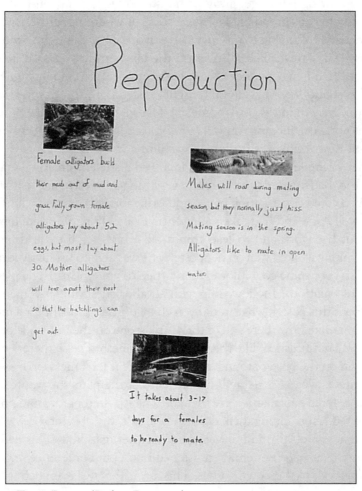

Figure 7–4a. Tory's Poster (Before Revision)

JESSICA: Why did you choose to research dolphins?

JULIE: I wanted to learn more facts.

SARAH: What main idea are you teaching us with your clay model?

JULIE: I want to show everyone what the dolphin looks like and point out all the body parts like the dorsal fin.

TEACHER: What is most important thing for us to learn?

JULIE: I want the other kids to know that dolphins are beautiful, but careless fishermen trap them in their nets. I watched a show and learned that other nets can be used. I was really inspired to learn more.

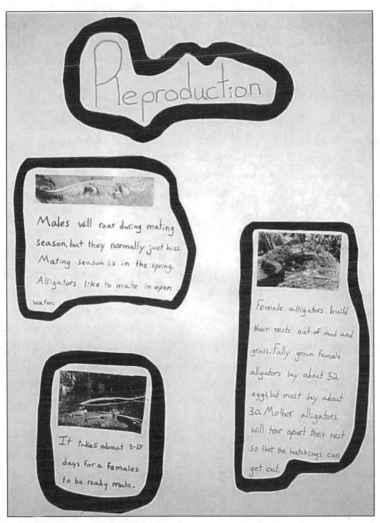

Figure 7–4b. Tory's Poster (After Revision)

A Reminder About Coaching Without Praise

As was discussed in the last chapter (see the section on the language of coaching), we must carefully choose the language we use to reinforce positives with students. I avoid using broad, general praise like "Good job!" and "I like your painting!" because it doesn't give students much specific feedback, and it can give them the idea that they are working to please me. I want to keep the power of the language focused on the work and the student: "How did you get the colors of your painting so close to the real colors of the fox you were studying? The colors make your fox look real."

Specific feedback based on observations gives students a real sense of what they are doing well. They also see that others appreciate their work, but the appreciation doesn't feel manipulative. This kind of language encourages students to feel good about their work and about themselves as a worker.

Other Examples of Teacher Language

I see you chose blue for the background of your poster. Why?
What are you most proud of when you look at this model?
Which element of your play do you think teaches the most?
How did you think of the rules for your game?

Timekeeping

As the timekeeper in the room, I must gauge the energy and enthusiasm levels as the project time progresses. Students should have at least a forty-five- to sixty-minute time slot for project work, depending on the age of the students, the time of year, and many other factors. As a general rule, any less than forty-five minutes at a time, and students spend too much time getting supplies ready and cleaning up for the work period to be productive. Too little time, and students have difficulty getting work done. Too much time, and students tend to drift and wander, not using their time to the fullest. The appropriate amount of time can vary from class to class and day to day. Some classes can handle a huge two-hour block, while others struggle to stay productive for more than thirty minutes. Though project work periods work well at any time, I find that these work periods are especially effective at the end of the day, when students need to be doing something active and independent. Students can sustain this kind of work even at times when independent writing and whole-class math lessons seem to fall flat.

I also play timekeeper on a grander scale. I must allot enough work periods for everyone to get nearly all of their work done. However, as some students begin to finish their projects, it is also important to set deadlines for the class as a whole. I know that there are some students who will never finish without a deadline. They will always think of another project to do or find something to fix on a project that is already done. For the students who need some extra time past the deadline, I once again make time before and after school available. Once, I even had three students come in to work on a Saturday!

Managing the Class

I always have to remember that my classroom management skills will be tested during this stage of work. Conflicts and problems will arise. Students will falter and make mistakes. A school assembly will come up and cancel out a work period. As the class manager, the teacher sets the tone of the classroom. High levels of stress when dealing with problems and conflicts will heighten student anxiety. If I am a constant, steady, reasonable voice in the class, the students will tend to lean in this direction as well. This doesn't mean that simply by remaining calm, a teacher will never have a student who is upset. What it does mean is that when a student is upset, the teacher will have a calming effect and will not throw gas on the fire.

A consistent and predictable approach to discipline will let students know they are safe and cared for. Class rules should be created by the students and teacher together to create a safe and positive learning environment. When students make mistakes, they need teachers who are fair and reasonable, ones who let logical consequences fall in order to help children learn. Children deserve to be treated respectfully. To learn more about an effective model for discipline that builds community and respect, check out the Responsive Classroom method of teaching. A few resources are cited at the end of this chapter.

Observing

There are times during this project-creation phase where I sit back and observe. I watch students interact with each other, recording specific things that I hear them saying. I watch how students attend to their work and how they solve problems. I have long since overcome the fear that if someone walks into my room and sees me sitting and watching the students, they will think I'm not working. Observation is one my most valuable sources of information about my students, and I must spend some part of each day engaged in recording what I see and hear.

Assessing

Assessment is ongoing during this phase of the research process. Every time I meet with a student to talk about their work, I'm doing some form of assessment. My goal is that students will have every available opportunity and resource to do polished, presentable work. This wasn't the way I first did this. I used to let students create projects with massive amounts of tape showing, incomplete content, and misspelled titles. I figured that I needed to let students do their own work, and that authentic student work would have these imperfections. I also counted on the assessment rubric (or other final assessment tool) to point out mistakes that were made. However, this never gave students a chance to practice getting better. The appropriate time to assess the spelling of a poster is while it is being made. Students now are required to do their posters in pencil and have me check their work for mistakes before they finish them off. That way, the assessment and corrections can happen while the work is still alive. Andy goes one step further. He requires that every poster be done on newsprint before students are even allowed to have their poster-board. He then coaches them through the specifics of polished poster work: spelling, punctuation, capitalization, color coordination, use of space, and so on.

Transition to Presentations

As students begin to wrap up their projects, it is time to shift the focus of the class toward presentations. When I first began working with students on research, I saw this as a clearly defined transition: first you create the projects, then you practice your presentations. Experience has taught me that this doesn't always work. Very often, students must start putting their presentation together in order to see if the projects they have created will work. Very often, as students begin work on their presentation, they realize that they need another project to help deliver some information. That is why I begin to discuss and have students plan their presentations near the end of the project creation time. The next chapter will get into the details of how this works.

Works Cited

Gardner, H. 1983. *Frames of Mind: The Theory of Multiple Intelligences.* New York: Basic Books.

Wood, C. 1997. *Yardsticks: Children in the Classroom Ages 4–14, a Resource for Parents and Teachers.* Greenfield, MA: Northeast Foundation for Children.

A Few Responsive Classroom Resources

Charney, R. 2002. *Teaching Children to Care.* Greenfield, MA: Northeast Foundation for Children.

Wood, C. 1997. *Yardsticks: Children in the Classroom Ages 4–14, a Resource for Parents and Teachers.* Greenfield, MA: Northeast Foundation for Children.

8

Presentations

Paul Revere: An Independent Presentation

Kelly peers into the classroom from the hallway and adjusts her tri-cornered hat. Her black jacket (a bit long—it's her father's) rests on the broomstick horse she is about to ride into class. Her classmates are aligned in chairs facing the front of the room, where Kelly has already placed her cardboard replica of the Boston Tea Party, a huge time line, and several posters. Though her classmates have all helped Kelly generate ideas for this presentation, so they know bits and pieces of what's coming, they wriggle in anticipation anyway. They are excited for the show. I get the video camera set, point it at the doorway to our classroom, press *record*, and give the thumbs-up sign to Kelly.

Kelly, a student who immerses herself in a project, begs to take parts of it home to work on at night, and she is meticulous about her final work. She has spent six weeks preparing for this moment. Paul Revere was her first choice of topics that came out of our study of conflict in American history. This research unit was the culmination of this study. She took copious notes at school during research periods in class, and when I directed the class to move to the project-making phase, she continued to gather more information during indoor recesses and at home for extra homework (her idea, not mine). Though we spent over two weeks working on projects in school, she often took projects home at night to do extra work. During the final couple of weeks, we spent a lot of time as a class preparing our presentations and practicing with each other. Kelly also practiced at night in front of her family. Her classmates knew how much time and effort she had invested and were eager to see the final results.

"The British are coming! The British are coming! The British are coming!" Kelly gallops into the classroom crying her warning. She races to the front of the room and faces the class. "The British are coming! Why are you just sitting there? Why don't you do

99

something? Come on!" she urges. The class giggles nervously and looks from side to side, unsure if they are really supposed to move. Kelly lets the tension hang for a moment and then continues, "Oh . . . are you Kelly's class? She told me to meet her here for a presentation about me. Since she's not here, I guess I'll do it for her. Hi. As you have probably figured out, I'm Paul Revere . . . Hey! Look at this! Kelly just happens to have a time line of my life right here. I guess I'll start by going through it with you."

Let's take a moment here to think about the emotional risk Kelly is taking. Fifth grade is certainly the transition year for most kids, where they become more invested in what their peers think and less inclined to seek explicit adult approval. Better to be cool than the teacher's pet. And here she is, dressed up like Paul Revere and delivering her presentation to her class.

Kelly/Paul Revere proceeds to share her time line with the class. The time line is a requirement of this project, no matter what facet of conflict in U.S. history the kids chose. This time line represents a lot of work on her part, as her class well knows. She struggled with layout issues once she moved away from the rough draft and began her final draft. She realized that she had too much information to fit on a regular-sized posterboard. During a peer conference, she got the idea of using two posterboards taped end to end to lengthen her time line to fit everything on it. This part of her presentation takes about three minutes; she moves into a straight lecture, simply delivering information.

"Now let's move on to something more fun," Kelly continues, having finished teaching some of the most important elements of Revere's life. "Next, I'd like to show you a reenactment of the Boston Tea Party. Please turn your seats so you are facing the boat." Off to the side of the presentation space is a bench that is part of our circle area. The bench is on its side, and taped to the front of it is a six-foot-long cardboard cutout of a ship. Kelly has several shoeboxes inside the ship, and as she explains how the Sons of Liberty disguised themselves as Mohawk Indians and threw the tea into Boston Harbor, she begins dumping the shoeboxes over the side of the ship. They are filled with construction-paper tea leaves that cascade onto the carpet.

"Now I'd like to get you all moving," she announces. "Everybody stand up and get ready to sing! Here's a copy of a song I wrote about Paul Revere's midnight ride, to the tune of 'Mary Had a Little Lamb.' Take a minute to look at the words, and then we'll all sing it together."

Talk about emotional risk? Here are a bunch of eleven-year-olds, standing together, about to sing a version of "Mary Had a Little Lamb"! And do you know what—they don't even bat an eye. In fact, they're quite used to this sort of thing by this point in the presentation schedule. One of the other requirements of this unit was that everyone had to use at least five of Howard Gardiner's multiple intelligences, and many students chose music as a way of teaching information. In fact, one of the students in this class has Down's syndrome, and he had the class get up and dance to a piece of music about his topic, and the kids cared enough about him and trusted each other enough that they were able to dance for three minutes, standing in a circle while he strummed away on an air guitar!

"Now we're going to play a game. We're going to play Group Charades, so count around the circle into five groups." The class breaks up into the groups, goes to different areas of the room, and waits for Kelly to give them their parts to act out. Once assigned, each group gets about two minutes to quickly come up with their skit and practice before rejoining in the presentation area. "Okay, group one, you act out Paul Revere being a silversmith." She moves to the next group; "You guys show the Tea Party." She continues around the room until each group has something to act out, and then the performances begin.

Kids in the room nearly fall out of their seats raising their hands to guess one another's skits. I had stressed that the games in their presentations should engage the audience, keep the presentation lively, and most important, should reinforce the content they are teaching. Group Charades is one of the favorites, and Kelly is right on with this one: each topic reinforces the content.

The second-to-last part of her presentation is the writing piece that everyone had to include. Kelly's was particularly intriguing. She wrote a poem by Paul Revere from beyond the grave, lamenting that he is only famous for his midnight ride when he was so much more: silversmith, Son of Liberty, husband, father, and so on. The poem is quite moving and shows not only the amount of information Kelly learned, but the depth with which she thought about her subject.

The conclusion for everyone's presentation was the same. Each student had to explain what they thought their central figure would have thought about our essential question: Is it ever okay to fight? Then they had to give their own answer to the same question.

"And now for the last part of my presentation. I think Paul Revere would say that it is okay to fight, but only in extreme cases. He thought it was right to fight against the British, but in general, he was a peaceful man. He loved his family and spent a lot of time with his children. He would say that sometimes you need to stand up for what you believe in and sometimes that means fighting.

"And now for what I think. I guess I would agree. I don't think that it's right to fight with your brothers and sisters, and kids shouldn't fight on the playground. Also, I think that wars are wrong, and we should all figure out better ways to solve arguments. But, sometimes, you have to fight for what you believe in. So that's what I think about whether or not it's right to fight.

"I'm ready for questions and comments."

We always end our presentations with questions and comments. This takes a lot of preparation and practice. The purpose of questions and comments is to ask the presenter clarifying or deeper questions about their learning and to find out about their learning process. It is important that the feedback stay positive and constructive.

> Many hands shoot up at once. John is the first to be called on. "How did you think to write that poem about Paul Revere?" Kelly answers, "All you ever hear about Paul Revere is his midnight ride, and that's all I really knew when I started studying him, but then I learned all of this other stuff. He was a father with something like eighteen kids. He was a silversmith. I wondered if he would be mad if people only knew him for that one ride."
>
> Garrett is next. "I really liked the way you dressed up as Paul Revere. It made me pay more attention, even when you were just telling information." Kelly responds, "Thanks. I thought it might keep everyone more awake if I dressed up."

Other questions and comments follow. How did you make the tea leaves? Your time line ended up turning out really well. The two posters worked well. What was the most interesting thing you learned about Paul Revere?

> After a few minutes, when Kelly is ready to end the questions and comments portion, she concludes. "I learned a lot about Paul Revere, and I hope you enjoyed this presentation. I'm ready for the next presentation." The class applauds, several students jump up to help her put away her work, and the rest of the class gets up for a stretch and a quick snack before the next presentation.

It's a magical moment when students put on their presentations. It takes structure and planning to make these presentations come together in the end. This chapter will be devoted to the process of teaching children how to plan and conduct effective presentations and how to assess the final products once they are complete. The process can be broken down into four steps:

1. Students plan their presentations.
2. Students practice their presentations.
3. Students give their presentations.
4. Teacher and students assess presentations.

Planning the Presentations

Once students have completed most of their projects, it's time to start thinking about how to show off all of their hard work. There are many ways to help students plan their presentations.

Like every other part of this process, presentations were a bit of a free-for-all when I first began doing them with students. I simply said, "Okay, everyone. You need to give a presentation to the class. Make sure you plan it out well!" Some students seemed to be able to do this with little or no instruction, but many floundered as they tried to follow my vague advice ("Make sure you plan it out well!") without any real idea of what that meant. Come to think of it, did I have any real idea what that meant?

Modeling

If I have been doing a research project right along with my students, then I will model my own planning for them. I put my notes, presentation requirements, and projects onto a table and have the class crowd around. I think aloud as I decide on a good order for my projects. "Should I do the game first to get everyone interested, or will that be better later on, to give the class a chance to move in the middle of the presentation?" I struggle with the best way to introduce and conclude my presentation. "Is it best to end with my quiz, or would this be the best place for the question-and-answer session I'd like to do?" I make sure to emphasize that at the end I will take questions and comments from the audience. Above all, I model how I need to write down all of this thinking so that I remember how I set everything up.

The importance of modeling for students cannot be emphasized enough. This kind of teaching is like a master-apprentice model of instruction and is powerful for the learner. Students get a chance to see what the process looks like, and they get to ask questions about it before they go off to work on their own. Modeling gives them a clear idea of what they should do.

Using Planning Sheets

When I first began doing research with students, I didn't have them use any kind of formal planning sheet. However, after a few times through the process I began to think that about four of my students might benefit from some sort of organizational tool to help them plan. Their presentations lacked any kind of cohesiveness. They forgot introductions and conclusions, transition phrases were weak at best, and students seemed to randomly jump from one project to the next. ("And now I'll show you my diorama. . . . I guess I'll show my time line next . . .") I decided these kids could use a planning sheet. I was wrong. All of my students could use a planning sheet. Even students who seemed organized without one benefited from having a place to plan their presentations. The plan on page 104 is just one example of how they might look.

Watching Former Students' Presentations

For years, I have videotaped student presentations and saved them in my classroom. I have a large collection that I can pull off the shelf to show to current students. Kids love to see other kids' presentations. Not only do they get to think

Presentation Plan

Name _____ Topic _____

Introduction _____

_____

_____

Project #1 _____ Main Idea _____

Transition Phrase _____

_____

Project #2 _____ Main Idea _____

Transition Phrase _____

_____

Project #3 _____ Main Idea _____

Transition Phrase _____

_____

Conclusion _____

_____

_____

about strategies for putting together their own presentations, but they also love the sense of history that the videotapes create. They love to hear about how old the videotaped student is now and what they were like. (Think back to the story about Mason remembering Emily's presentation so vividly!)

Practicing Presentations

I find that the planning for the presentations usually takes a day or two, and then students are ready to practice. Students who plan quickly begin practicing while others are still in the planning phase. Often, the students who plan *too* quickly discover through their practicing that they've left something out, so they jump back to the planning stage.

Practicing Alone

The first couple of times students run through their presentation, I encourage them to do it on their own. They find a designated spot in the room for presentation rehearsals or an out-of-the-way nook of the classroom and try their presentation alone. This gives them a first chance to say the words out loud, practicing tone, volume, and transitions. If there are any gaps in their presentation, they often show up here, and the students can fix them up.

Practicing with a Peer

Another way to practice is to present to a peer. This might be a classmate, a friend from another classroom, or even a reading buddy from a younger grade. My students love to share their work with their second-grade reading buddies, and the reading buddies are equally excited. Students now get a chance to see how someone else reacts to their presentations, and very often, these dry runs reveal what is working well and what needs to be improved. One of my colleagues, a second-grade teacher, has found some portable display boards on wheels that she rolls out when it's time for students to practice with each other. They wheel them right into the hallway and set up their presentations on the boards to practice with a friend. It's fun to watch other students, passing by on their way to art class or lunch, trying to peek around the boards to see what's going on behind them!

Practicing at Home

Sometimes it might be appropriate to give students the homework assignment of practicing their presentations for a family member or babysitter. This can give them a fresh perspective on their work. It is also a nice way for parents to see the kind of work they have been doing in class. There is a caution here: I must always make sure that parents understand their role in the process. I send a note home with this assignment, letting parents know that they can offer advice about the presentation itself but may not tamper with the projects or the other work pieces. As was mentioned previously, it can be tempting for some parents to fix spelling or suggest a new project, and before the student knows what has happened, they're watching their dad construct a new model for their presentation that needs seventeen different power tools and a building permit.

Watching a Teacher Presentation

Once my students are nearing the end of their planning and practicing stages, it is time for me to model a presentation. I get up in front of the class and give my presentation. Before I begin, I direct them to look for the main objectives that we have set for the presentation. "Check out my eye contact. Also see if I included the basic *who, what, where, when, why,* and *how* information about my topic." They all have the assessment tool that we're using, and they watch and then assess my presentation. After we have finished, we debrief, and students get to reflect on the presentation, asking questions and making comments.

I also point out that I get nervous at the beginning of my presentation, just like they do. It helps kids deal with their anxieties if they know that adults get nervous in front of a group as well. I then share my strategies for coping with my nervousness. "When I'm nervous, it's usually because I'm worried that I won't do well. I get too focused on what other people will think about my work. To try to help that, I'm going to focus on the information I want to tell instead of worrying about how good it is. I know that when I'm nervous, I tend to fiddle with my watch or my wedding ring. To try to limit that, I'm going to hold this pointer stick that I will use to highlight information on posters. At the end of the presentation, let me know how I did."

Traditional Presentations

Students now get to finally present their work. They are excited, nervous, and eager to share their learning. The presentation format that is most traditional and effective is the one in which students stand up in front of the class and conduct an oral presentation. Since this is the one that we use most often, Mike and I decided to write the majority of the chapter with this style in mind, though we do give some examples later on of some other presentation formats that we have found to be very successful. In order for any presentation, regardless of style and format, to go smoothly, there are several considerations to keep in mind.

Creating a Reasonable Schedule

There are many different ways to structure a class set of presentations. I might take an entire day and do nothing but presentations. Fun snacks served by parents and lots of mini recesses and game breaks between presentations keep the day lively and festive. It is exhausting, but feels like a true celebration.

Another way to present, especially if many of the presentations are long, is to stretch them out over a week or two. Three or four presentations a day can be plenty if the presentations are thirty minutes each. Students who need an extra day or two to prepare have the option of choosing a later presentation date so they are ready when it is their turn.

In some classrooms that I know, the research process is an ongoing part of the year, and students are all working at their own pace. They are independent enough that they can each work on their own project in their own time, and the teacher coaches them individually throughout the process. In this case, whenever a student is ready to present, they sign up with the teacher for a presentation date and the class gets a special treat that day.

Choosing an Audience

Most often, the audience for these presentations is the class itself. Students love to see one another get up and show off all of the hard work they have done, and because they have all worked together and given each other advice, they each have a sense of pride about one another's work. However, there are many other audiences to consider.

I try to schedule presentations so that students can ask other adults or students to come see them. They invite former teachers, counselors, special education and remedial tutors, administrators, siblings, best friends from other rooms, and so on. It is really fun to get other people from the school to come in and share in the students' celebrations of learning. As an added bonus, other teachers get excited about the process and want to learn more about it.

Parents or other friends and family members are another wonderful audience. Sometimes we send invitations home for families so they know when the child is presenting and can try to take an hour off from work. Grandparents, neighbors, and video cameras often come too. Another great way to celebrate with parents and other family members is to have a nighttime celebration at the school. If students have all done individual projects, they can set them up around the cafeteria or gymnasium and present them all at once. This requires a lot of space, since twenty simultaneous presentations can make quite a bit of noise.

Audience Participation

When the audience is composed of the students in the class, wonderful skills can be taught and practiced during presentations. I have often spent several class periods during the time leading up to presentations focusing on good audience skills. Just like anything else, these skills need to be modeled and role-played by students before the presentations begin. I keep the expectations of the audience high, and expect students to be active learners during the presentations.

Audience Skills to Teach	
• Active listening	• Noticing
• Note taking	• Taking a quiz
• Thinking	• Making relevant comments
• Asking relevant questions	• Sitting respectfully
• Learning new ideas	• Many more . . .

Questions and Comments

Each presentation ends the same way. Once the student has concluded their presentation, they say, "I'm ready for questions and comments." The responsibility of the audience is to be ready with thoughtful, positive feedback about the presentation. This gives presenters an immediate response and the audience the opportunity to show their appreciation for everyone's hard work.

Like everything else, questions and comments must be modeled and practiced. I teach students to use the nonjudgmental language of "I noticed" instead of "I liked." I encourage students to be specific in their feedback. "I noticed that because you dressed up like Paul Revere, I really got a picture of what he looked like. The hat and the clothes were very realistic," instead of "I like the way you dressed up."

It recently became apparent to me that by the end of the school year, my students had begun to emulate me when it came to the questions and comments at the end of a presentation. My deliberate use of language, my voice inflections, even my mannerisms were beginning to emerge in my children. Alex, a boy who struggled with commenting on presentations at the beginning of the year, was a perfect example. After a small group's presentation, he raised his hand to make a comment. Resting his clipboard in one hand and scratching his head with the pen in his other hand (looking remarkably like his teacher), he leaned forward a bit, paused, and began. "I'm wondering what topic you plan to research next, but before you answer that, I also want to hear from each of you a brief explanation about what it was like to work with the others." Alex looked back at me for a brief second with a slight smile, and then turned his head to readdress the presenters. He knew.

Applause

Every presenter deserves applause after they have taken a huge risk by getting up in front of an audience and sharing their learning. Most of the time, we use straight clapping, but there are other fun ways to show appreciation as well. A "Standing O" is when the whole class stands up and makes a big O with their arms over their heads. The "Seal of Approval" is a clap with arms extended and crossed, accompanied by the barking sound of seals. As the year progresses and we add new forms of applause to our class repertoire, we keep a chart of them listed in the room. Then, students can choose the form of applause they receive after their presentations. The list on page 110 shows some of the various applauses and celebrations that Mike and I have gathered over the years.

Other Presentation Formats

This chapter began with Kelly's presentation on Paul Revere. This presentation style, where one student, who has studied one topic, presents his or her work to an audience, is the most common format we have used for research presentations. However, there are many, many others that can also be effective. Here are a few.

Individual Presentations, Two Locations

It is a humid afternoon in May, and anxious third graders sit in their seats as parents gather in the circle area awaiting instructions. I quickly explain that half the class will be traveling to the computer lab, where they will share their hyper-studio projects, and the other half will remain in the room and share their wall space work. The computer-lab group lines up, is quickly joined by their parents, and heads off. The children remaining in the room direct their parents to their display spaces. A productive buzz fills the room as students and parents begin talking about the display spaces. Becca's three-year-old brother breaks into a tantrum and

Applauses and Celebrations

Seal of Approval: Clap your hands while your arms are extended and crossed, and bark like a seal.

Standing O: Everyone stands up while making a big O over their heads with their arms.

Silent Cheer: The class stands and yells, screams, and claps wildly (but silently).

Round of Applause: While clapping your hands together, rotate them in circles in front of your body.

Standing Ovation: Everyone stands while clapping.

Kiss Your Brain: Kiss your hand, then touch your hand to your head.

2-4-6-8: Do the cheer: "2-4-6-8, who do we appreciate? Brian!" (any name).

Two Thumbs Up and Give It Some Steam: Put your two thumbs up, and make a hissing-teakettle noise.

Fireworks: Begin with hands spread wide and fingers closed, then slowly bring them together making a hissing noise (this is the fuse); when they meet, clap, keep the hands together and stream them up straight saying "whoop" (this is the firework going up in the air); once high in the air, clap hands together and let the fingers wiggle on the way down, saying "ahhhh."

Fonzie: Put both thumbs up and say "Aaaaaay."

Cowboy Cheer: Say "Yee-haw" while circling a lasso in the air.

Fantastic: Spray and wipe the window.

Elvis: Everyone stands and says, "Thank you. Thank you very much."

Austin Powers: Everyone stands and says, "Groovy, baby!"

Oompa Loompa: Every one stands and sings (to the tune of the Oompa Loompa song from *Charlie and the Chocolate Factory*) "Oompa Loompa, doompa-di-do. This is a fun way to thank you!"

Clam Clap: Place hands together at the palms and clap, keeping the palms together.

Mitten Clap: Clap without letting your hands touch.

Crab Clap: Make claws with your hands and clap your thumbs and fingers together.

Alligator Clap: Open arms wide (like alligator jaws) and clap together.

briefly gains the attention of the visitors, but not for long. They quickly turn their focus back to the work at hand and the room settles down. I eavesdrop and hear Page's father ask her how she knew all this stuff about red-eyed tree frogs. She opens her folder and pulls out her note cards and graphic organizer to show how she organized her information.

I scan the room and see that none of the other children have opened their folders; they're focused on their display spaces, so I make a quick announcement to encourage all the students in the class to do what Page did and instruct them to pull out their folders and share the *process* with their parents.

Meanwhile, down the hall in the computer lab, the other half of the class shares their PowerPoint presentations. These have been the main focus of computer class instruction for the past month, and the finished products are complete with music backgrounds and smooth transitions. Some students have even embedded video clips with the help of the computer teacher, a skill that I hope to learn myself.

After about fifteen minutes, we switch groups. Parents and students in the classroom go to the computer lab, and the parents and kids from the computer lab proudly return to the room. Everyone is eager to see the other half of the presentations. As parents pass each other in the doorway, one of them whispers to me, "I can't believe there's more!"

Class Play

One year we produced a class play during a thematic research unit on the Pilgrims. Students chose which of five topics they were most interested in studying. One group learned about England in the early 1600s, another group focused on the voyage, one concentrated on learning about the arrival, and the final group studied the survival of the Pilgrims. After gathering data, groups wrote their own lines, studied them, and performed them in a play for parents and peers before beautiful large backdrops they created as a team. Students assimilated an unbelievable amount of information into the play, and truly enjoyed presenting their learning in this format.

Evening Group Presentation

Mike once had a celebration evening with a fifth-grade class who had just completed team research projects on ecosystems from around the world. Each team created a scene from their ecosystem in a different area of the room. Blue and purple tissue paper covered the lights in the Arctic, vines and tropical trees covered the loft in the rain forest, another area of the room had the wavy grass of the Serengeti Plain, the hallway was transformed into a desert, and a coral reef scene was painted on the windows. Relatives showed up in droves, and seventy-five people crammed into the classroom to watch all of the presentations. It was a truly magical night where parents came to support their children's learning!

Carousel Walk

Another way to have students share individual work is through a carousel walk. Students set up their work in a large space like the cafeteria or gymnasium, science-fair style. The audience enters the room, chooses a starting point, and is given a time limit to visit each display. I call out, "Switch!" or ring a chime or a bell to signal for the audience to move. This makes sure that all presenters get equal audience time. I have also had the audience just mill around at their own pace, but I've found that invariably, some students have crowds of people and others spend too much time sitting by themselves, so I prefer to structure the time spent at each display.

Since so many people are traveling at once, it is hard to have much in the way of questions and comments with this structure, so people travel with sticky notes. If they can't ask the presenter their question or make their comment as they walk, they jot down what they want to say and stick it to the display area. Presenters can then get more feedback and respond to questions later.

Individual Sharing for a Different Purpose

A Summer Literacy Institute graduate student from Mike's class designed this format. Susan teaches at an international school in London, and she planned a six-week unit to help her students gain a sense of place. Since her students come from all over the world, many of them don't have a sense of belonging to a place in the world. They might have been born in India to Italian and Lebanese parents but have spent much of their life in Germany. Susan said that her main goal at the beginning of each year is to help her students connect with each other and gain a sense of community. So in her research unit each student researched a place in the world with which they had a strong connection. It might be where they were born or where they spend the summers with their grandparents. It might be another place where they lived for a while. As long as they had a strong connection to the place, it would qualify. They researched this place to teach the class about it and themselves. The presentations were just for each other and became the ultimate get-to-know-each-other activity.

Individual Sharing for Yet Another Purpose

Todd was another student from that same graduate class. He teaches ninth-grade literacy, and every year his students read and explore *The Iliad*. He wanted to give his students some background knowledge about this challenging text, so he came up with about thirty different people, places, and things from the book that his students could research. Because this was an introduction to a book, he wanted the research to be quick, so the whole research unit was about two weeks. Students chose a topic, learned about it, and came up with a quick presentation to share with the class. I had never thought of using the research process as a quick introduction for a unit, but this clearly made sense. His students all knew a little bit more about this tough book before they dove in, and they supported each other with this knowledge as they read.

And these are just a few presentation possibilities. So many factors influence what presentation fits a particular research unit: time, space, availability of parents and other audience members, age of the students and their experience with research, curricular demands, and on and on and on. . . . Let's also not forget the special talents and comforts of teachers. If a teacher is excited about producing a play, using music, creating a website, or making a huge class mural, those talents and passions should be harnessed for the good of the class. The possibilities are limitless.

Assessments

My major emphasis in the assessment process is to highlight what went well during the unit. It can be tempting to spend lots of time with students pointing out what they could have done better. When I was in school the majority of the assessments I endured seemed primarily focused on what I did wrong. Although finding room for improvement is a vital part of the assessment process, it should not be the focus. (I pick one or two skills at a time to have a young researcher work on.) Research has shown that when students are aware of the progress they are making and can antic- ipate having some success, they are more motivated (Allington and Cunningham 1996; Stainbeck and Stainbeck 1992). The more we can highlight the strengths and aptitudes that our students demonstrate, the more excited they are about learning.

When I first began using the research process, my assessment sheets were often very complicated or overwhelming. I tried to give feedback about way too much. In fact, I often assessed students' projects, content, and presentations all at once in the end. As I have used more ongoing assessments during research work, and stu- dents have created posters, skits, clay models, and other projects that are truly pol- ished, I have no longer needed to give lots of written feedback about the quality of students' research work. For one thing, this kind of assessment, done after the pro- jects are complete, is a bit late; there isn't a chance to fix any mistakes at this point. And in the end, what was I actually doing? Did I really expect that a student, two months after receiving feedback that his poster had too much tape showing, would use that feedback to create a more polished poster? Now, when assessing student presentations, I focus on assessing the *presentations* themselves.

First, I must choose the kind of assessment(s) that will be used. This depends on the overall theme or topic of the research unit (if there is one), the needs of a class, or the needs of individual students. There are times when I use just one assessment and others when I use several. The following are some assessment methods that I have found particularly effective.

Rubrics

Rubrics are effective for pinpointing specific aspects of students' work. They are easy to read and allow for various levels of competency to be recorded. The key to an effective rubric is that students can understand the language and format that are used. The rubric on page 115 is one example.

Narratives

One of my favorite forms of assessment is a narrative. It is more personal and easier to individualize than a rubric, though it certainly takes more time. As I watch students' presentations, I take careful notes so that I will be able to give specific feedback; specificity is the key to a good narrative. Narratives allow me to give a truly individualized assessment for each child, focusing on strengths and areas to work on, regardless of ability.

The language I use in a narrative is just as important as the language I use face-to-face with students. It needs to be as clear and as nonjudgmental as possible. The following narrative shows how this might sound:

Dear Justin,

Your presentation on Abraham Lincoln was well organized. You had a solid introduction and conclusion, and the order of your projects made sense. It was logical to begin with his childhood, then teach us about his early political life, and finally give details about his presidency.

Your presentation skills are becoming more polished. You made eye contact with the class while you gave your presentation, and your voice was much more clear than your last presentation on dolphins. You still need to work on keeping your body still while speaking. You tended to shift from foot to foot.

Overall, the class seemed interested and engaged during your presentation, and judging by the questions and comments at the end, I'd say we all learned a lot!

Checklists

Checklists are similar to rubrics, though they are more simplistic. The list on page 116 shows the skills and requirements that students are working on with a space to check off or date when the skill is accomplished. Lists like this can be helpful when

Rubric				
	This skill is **beginning.**	This skill is **developing.**	This skill is **secure.**	This skill shows a high level of **mastery.**
The presenter made strong and steady **eye contact** with the audience.				
The presenter's **body language** was expressive, not distracting.				
The presenter's **voice** was an appropriate volume.				
Smooth **transitions** were used during the presentation.				
The **audience** was kept **active** during the presentation.				

Presentation Skills Demonstrated

❑   solid introduction

❑   eye contact made with audience

❑   clear speaking voice

❑   body faced audience

❑   body language was expressive

❑   audience was active

❑   smooth transitions were used

❑   logical organization

❑   15–30 minutes in length

❑   solid conclusion

there are lots of skills and objectives and students have some choices about which ones they are working on. I also enjoy the less-judgmental nature of checklists. They are fairly simple. Either a skill, competency, or attribute was shown or it wasn't.

A Combination of Assessments

Often, I want the whole class to focus on several key skills or concepts that we have all been working on, but I still want to give students more specific feedback about their work. In order to do this, I create a checklist or rubric that has space at the bottom for notes or a narrative. The example on page 118 is from an unthemed unit. The topics ranged from Komodo dragons to Hitler to baseball. It was the last research presentation for a group of fourth graders who had been with me through third and fourth grade. As a class, we brainstormed all of the skills that we had been practicing for two years and came up with a list of five attributes that we all wanted to have on our checklists. Then, I had each child take home and watch the videotape of all their previous presentations. They had to come up with a list of a few things they did well and a few things they wanted to do better. These became their individual goals for the last presentation. I left space at the bottom for notes. After their last presentation, each student brought their tape home, watched their presentation, and filled out a copy of their assessment form. I also filled out a copy. Then we compared the two in a conference, discussing how the presentation went.

Some Thoughts About Grading

Many teachers and schools rely on letter grades as their final word on the quality of students' work. Many of us were trained as children to accept the letter grade as the sole indicator of our performance. If you are required to use letter grades on the report cards you send home, or if you find them an effective means of communicating learning to parents, then rubrics, narratives, observations, and projects can all inform your grading so that grades are fair and consistent. It is important, however, to examine for a moment why letter grades are often an inappropriate way to assess this kind of work.

First of all, letter grades end discussion. They are meant to be the final word on a piece of work. The presentation was a B or a C. Students accept them, happily or unhappily, and then move on. Once, my students begged me to give them letter grades on their project evaluations. Reluctantly, I agreed. I wrote one-page narratives for each of them, highlighting what I felt they had done well and what could be improved for next time, and at the bottom of the narrative, I wrote their letter grade. Nearly every single student did the exact same thing when they got their assessment. They quickly scanned down to the bottom to see their letter grade and then put their narrative away without reading it.

Presentation Assessment

Name _____ Topic _____

❏ The presentation was 10–15 minutes long.

❏ The presenter used good eye contact.

❏ The presenter used effective body position.

❏ The presenter used smooth transitions between parts of the presentation.

❏ The presenter gave his or her opinion about whether or not it was right to fight in the conflict they studied.

Narrative _____

_____

_____

_____

Goal for Future Research Work

_____

_____

_____

Also, letter grades are often too subjective. What is a B+ presentation? What's the difference between a C and a C–? I heard a story once of an experiment done at a conference for high school English teachers. All of the participants were given a paper to grade. The participants read the papers, graded them, and passed them in. That one single paper received every grade on the scale from A+ through F.

What about those students who need to learn to deal with letter grades, you ask? True, most students in middle school and high school are assessed primarily through letter grades, so it may be tempting to "prepare students" by giving letter grades in earlier years. The following email that I got from a student recently illustrates pretty well how students adjust to letter grades when they get them and how these research projects help get students ready.

> Hi! Its Becca! How is your family? I'm in the 7th grade now—whew! I'm doing ok. I had to do a science project/presentation a couple weeks ago. After everyone presented, mine and Kelly's were the best of 16 kids. Don't think that you're a mean old rotten teacher for making us present for 15 to 30 minutes. My science teacher made us do it for 5 to 7 minutes but most peoples were less than that. I learned allot from you like how to type a really good report and to organize information easily. All thanks to you, I got an A+! I hope to hear back from you soon!

Self-Assessments and Goal Setting

A powerful way to help students learn how to be more self-reflective is to have them fill out an assessment themselves. If I write a narrative, students write a narrative. If I fill out a checklist or rubric, so do they. I have them do their own assessment before I hand mine back, and then we compare to see what we had in common and what differed. These quick conferences are powerful tools.

I also require students to set goals for each new research presentation. They review previous presentations and figure out what one or two things they would like to improve. Do they want to make better eye contact with the audience or speak more clearly? Did their posters keep falling over during their last presentation? If so, how could they keep them more stable this time? It can be difficult for students to remember how everything about their presentation went. Realistically, how would they be able to rate their quality of eye contact without seeing themselves? That is why videotaping is so important. Every year, students get a videotape for recording each presentation. Then, they can take their tape home (or watch it in school if they don't have a VCR) and use it to self-assess and set goals. This is also another great way to have parents see the presentations if they can't make it into the classroom easily. At the end of the year, students take their tapes home.

A Final Word

Have you ever been backstage with a group of middle school or high school actors just before or right after a play? The level of energy and excitement is through the roof. This is similar to the scene during a presentation week in the classroom. The same nervous energy precedes each presentation, and the flood of happy relief accompanies the end. I have never seen such energy during math lessons, or even really fun science experiments. There is simply something astounding about students having the power and control of their own class for their presentation. Each student has become an expert in a field of their choice and has the chance to teach others what they have learned, a moving and powerful experience. Though the presentations take a lot of planning and class time, they are the culmination to all of the hard work and struggle of the previous weeks and are truly worth it!

Works Cited

Allington, R. L., and P. M. Cunningham. 1996. *Schools That Work: Where All Children Read and Write*. New York: Addison-Wesley.

Stainbeck, S., and W. Stainbeck. 1992. *Curriculum Considerations in Inclusive Classrooms: Facilitating Learning for All Students*. Baltimore: Brookes Publishers.

9

Goal Setting

Student Goal Setting

Jimmy chooses a "round of applause" from his audience and beams with pride as he begins to take his posters and projects away from the presentation area. "Congratulations, Jimmy! How do you think it went?" I ask. "Well, I taught everybody a lot and I think I kept everyone active, but next time, I want to figure out how to keep my posters from falling down while I present," he states.

Like all good teachers, students finish their presentations already thinking about what they want to improve next time. Once students have had a chance to reflect on their work, it is time to set goals for future presentations. They are usually eager to start another project right away and have all kinds of ideas for possible topics and projects they would like to try. It is important to capitalize on this enthusiasm while the previous project is still fresh in their minds.

There are several ways to gather information about students' goals for future presentations. I almost always have some sort of conference with students and ask them what they think they did well and what they might do differently the next time around. Students might also fill out a survey, answering questions about strengths, refinements, and questions they have. If presentations were videotaped, students can watch their video to help with goal setting. The important thing is to get students thinking about what they did well and what they want to get better at. When the next research project is under way, students should get a chance to review and revisit the goals that they set and use these to create more effective presentations.

I find that students struggle with goal setting at the beginning of a school year, especially if they have had few chances to be self-reflective in earlier grades. This is an especially tough task for students who are used to teachers' grading and assessing everything for them. I remember one girl who came into my classroom

121

halfway through third grade. Every time she did a piece of work, she would approach me and say, "Mr. A, is it good? Do you like it?" When I turned the question back to her, "What do you think about it?" she had no idea how to respond. In her previous school, her teacher had always told her what she thought about her work without giving Katie the chance to. We worked on this the rest of the year. She had many chances to self-assess academically, and I rarely answered her "How did I do?" questions with straight answers. I think it's important to note that this was an explicit goal I had for her, and I made sure to share it with her parents. I moved to fourth grade with her class, and I clearly remember a moment from one of the first days of school. She had just finished her "Hopes and Dreams" goal-setting sheet for the beginning of the year, and she came up to me and said, "I worked really hard on this, Mr. A. The handwriting is neat, I tried to spell every word right, and I used lots of good color." When I asked her if she remembered how hard that kind of thinking had been for her last year, she smiled and said that she did. Then she bounced back to her seat smiling all the way.

As I write this, many students in my class are just now able to accurately self-assess. Several students who are overly critical of their own work are relaxing a bit and being a bit more realistic, and several of my students who were perfectly happy with sloppy handwriting and poor spacing on posters are voluntarily redoing work to make it look better. There are still several children who can't do this yet, but that's okay. We're moving on to fifth grade together next year, so we have time to work on it!

Teacher Goal Setting

It is just as important for me to reflect on the research process. What was I really pleased with as a leader of the research process? Maybe the students were really enthusiastic. Why? What enabled students to become excited and motivated? Perhaps the research itself went really well, and students learned valuable skills. How? What lessons in particular seemed most helpful? Teachers are often good at focusing on what didn't go well or what frustrated us. It is vitally important for me to focus on what went well with a unit. It gives me a base to work from for our next project.

Once the positives have been examined, it's time to look at areas that need refinement. Why was it that even though students gathered tons of facts, the projects they created seemed a little flat? Did they have enough time? Should I have tapped the resources of the art teacher? Why were a few presentations only three minutes long while others lasted more than thirty minutes? Should there be a time limit on the next one? Although many students gained lots of practice with nonfiction reading during their work, this reading was not directly assessed, so it's hard to tell how that practice paid off. How could I better assess a skill like that in the future? These kinds of questions and reflections lead me to stronger and more thoughtful teaching.

Just like I get my students talking with each other about their work, I need to do the same for myself. When two or three teachers combine their talents and energies into a group project with several classes together, the reflection process is powerful and exciting. Don Graves talks about the power of engaging in meaningful work and discussion with colleagues in his book *The Energy to Teach*. When teachers collaborate, we are more thoughtful and reflective, and we get energy together to take risks and improve our teaching. As I wrote in the introduction, the collaborative process of writing this book with Andy has been one of the most powerful activities of my career. The wonderful by-product has been that our teaching of research has become stronger as well. Each time we met and worked on the book, we took practical teaching strategies back to our own classrooms. The constant reflection that is required to write a book fueled our creativity in the classrooms and made our teaching that much better. I already have several goals for my next round of research projects based on the latest weekend session with Andy.

And Finally . . .

Let me warn you that if you ever choose to come and visit my classroom (or Andy's, for that matter), you will certainly see things happening that are not included in this book. When Andy and I first began talking together about the research process, we were at the beginning of our teaching careers and taking a course at Lesley College in Boston. The two-hour car rides from Connecticut and back every Wednesday night for a semester gave us the time needed to talk through this process, and the class itself became the first forum for us to publicly share our work on the research process. When we actually began to write the book, I had just married Heather and moved to New Hampshire; Andy was the proud father of a two-year-old and a two-month-old. His daughters are now eight and six, and my two children are four and two. The point is, it took a very long time for us to put this book together and polish it off. We would work furiously for several months and then put things down for a while. After a break of a few months, we'd go back to look at a chapter that had been written a year earlier and realize that it no longer matched the way we taught. Each year, this research process changes in our classrooms as we experiment with new ideas and discard ones that no longer fit our current thinking. Chances are, in a few more years, we'll look back at this book and wish we could revise and tweak it further. That's okay. In fact, it's one of the main points of this book: teaching and learning is an organic and dynamic process. It's messy at times, it's almost always hard, and if the learning is authentic, it is in a state of constant change. When my students come away from my classroom with the idea that learning is all about getting excited about an idea, taking chances, making mistakes, learning from them, and trying something new, than I consider myself an effective teacher. So, good luck. Try something, experiment, and let us know what you discover. We're always looking for new ideas!

Work Cited

Graves, D. 2001. *The Energy to Teach*. Portsmouth, NH: Heinemann.